$18.95

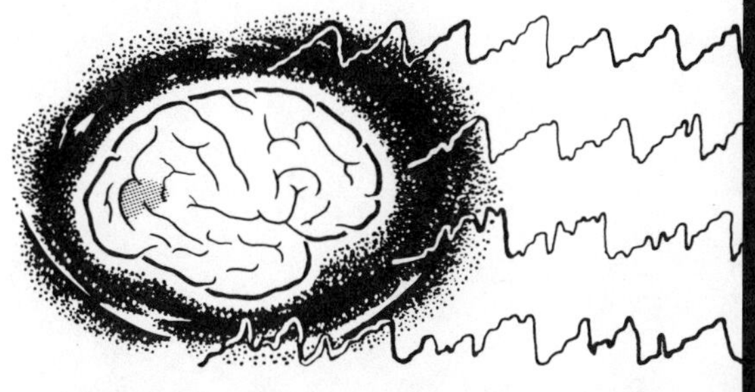

THE NEUROPSYCHOLOGY OF DEVELOPMENTAL READING DISORDERS

FOREWORD BY

HARRY A. WHITAKER

FRANCIS J. PIROZZOLO

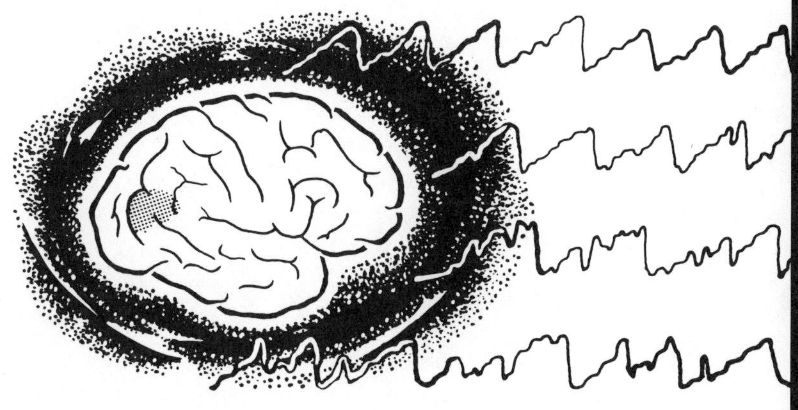

THE NEUROPSYCHOLOGY OF DEVELOPMENTAL READING DISORDERS

New York • London • Sydney • Toronto

Library of Congress Cataloging in Publication Data

Pirozzolo, Francis J
The neuropsychology of developmental reading disorders.

Bibliography: p.
Includes index.
1. Reading disability. 2. Neuropsychology.
I. Title.
RC394.W6P57 616.8'553 78-19752
ISBN 0-03-046121-9

PRAEGER PUBLISHERS,
PRAEGER SPECIAL STUDIES
383 Madison Avenue, New York, N.Y. 10017, U.S.A.

Published in the United States of America in 1979
by Praeger Publishers, Inc.
A Division of Holt, Rinehart and Winston, CBS, Inc.

9 038 987654321

Printed in the United States of America

To Dr. Joseph M. Wepman, who introduced me
to the field of human neuropsychology
and to the study of reading disability

FOREWORD
Harry A Whitaker

There are about 30,000 fibers in the auditory nerve and about 1,000,000 fibers in the optic nerve in man; clearly, the visual system is one of the most important components of our brains, just as vision is one of the most important features of human behavior. Our knowledge of the structural and functional aspects of vision was commented upon by James Hinshelwood at the turn of the century:

> The optical aspect of vision has long been studied with great attention. The anatomy, physiology, pathology, and physics of the eye have been investigated with the greatest care. The cerebral or mental aspect of vision, however, has not received the same attention. Yet the brain contributes quite as much to each visual act as the eye itself, and there are many visual defects, where the eye is perfectly healthy and where the lesion lies in the cerebral centres of vision. We are apt to forget that we see with our brains as well as with our eyes. (Letter-, Word-, and Mind-Blindness, 1899)

In the intervening three-quarters of a century we have corrected the balance somewhat. It is interesting to note, for example, that in the third revised edition of R. L. Gregory's Eye and Brain (1978) that more pages are devoted to perceptual/behavioral aspects of seeing than to the anatomical and physiological. But in terms of direct empirical quantification, it is likely the case that the balance of our knowledge will be structural in nature; we can light up the visual pathways of the brain with radioactively labeled 2-deoxyglucose, but for now the visual image has eluded such manipulations.

Reading must certainly rank as one of the more specialized features of visual processing, and obviously, a very important one. Although it merits only passing mention in Gregory's book, it has long been of major concern in neuropsychological investigations. Virtually all of the influential works on language and brain relationships since the 1890s have discussed reading and reading disorders. A common observation since that date is that reading disabilities may be impaired, both in the adult and in the developing child, in relative isolation from other language and speech impairments, and, significantly, in the context of an otherwise intact visual system. On the face of it, this is a rather striking observation which seems to suggest that (at least some) aspects of cognitive behavior are independent. However, such an analysis will only serve as an introduction to the problem because, as we all know, reading is an extremely complex behavior. An understanding of reading will entail, in microcosm so to speak, an understanding of brain and behavior in the broadest sense. Francis Pirozzolo is clearly aware of the multidisciplinary scope of research on dyslexia. In this book one will discover a number of his insights and contributions, based upon his research and clinical experience. By reading this book one will thereby gain some further understanding of the process which enabled the reader to do so.

PREFACE

Developmental dyslexia is the syndrome of unexpected reading failure. Many facts have been established about developmental dyslexia and the cognitive disabilities that correlate with this reading disturbance. Epidemiological observations have established that dyslexia is more prevalent in males than in females and that there is some reason to believe that it is influenced by heredity, but the precise nature of these relationships is unclear. Whether developmental reading disturbances are transmitted by a recessive gene or follow a dominant mode of inheritance is still a question that should be subjected to careful scrutiny.

Perhaps the most dismal reflection of the state of the art is the great disparity among estimates of the incidence of developmental dyslexia. A review of this literature reveals suggested frequencies as low as one in 500 and as high as one in three!

Many speculations as to the possible causes of reading failure have been extended but the etiology is still unknown. The definition of developmental dyslexia is also a source of great concern and confusion because it remains a definition by exclusion. Nevertheless, we think that careful distinction between children who are specifically retarded in reading acquisition and children who suffer from other intellectual, biological, emotional, or cultural handicaps will lead to both an acceptable definition and an understanding of the cause of the disorder. The condition can probably be best understood as a neurological entity. The neurological basis for the disorder has certainly not been established but, as the title of this book implies, the significance of neuropsychological findings is preeminent. One clinicopathological case report does exist (Drake 1968), that of a dyslexic child who died from a vascular malformation in the cerebellum. Autopsy revealed an atypical cortical gyral pattern with microgyria and pachygyria, as well as absence of the typical pattern of six well-differentiated layers of cortex. A cause and effect relationship cannot be inferred from this single case report, however.

Although, in general, research in developmental dyslexia is not characterized by an overabundance of clear thinking, the research selected to be reviewed here is quite scientifically sound. This research strongly suggests a neurological basis for developmental dyslexia. Quite clearly, developmental dyslexia poses a formidable challenge for neuropsychological research. Future investigations must continue to attack the difficult problems that have up until now had elusive solutions.

ACKNOWLEDGEMENTS

I am indebted to many colleagues who read and commented on various portions of this book and the studies on which it is based. Appreciation is expressed to Drs. Arthur Benton, D. Frank Benson, Ola A. Selnes, D. Wilson Hess, David Goldblatt, and David Taylor.

The completion of this book, protracted many weeks, would not have been possible without the encouragement and understanding of my editor, Dr. George Zimmar.

Very special thanks are due to Drs. Keith Rayner and Harry A. Whitaker, who have served as critics, advisors, and friends throughout all phases of the work described here. In addition to these contributions, Dr. Rayner did the strip chart recording for the auditory-linguistic dyslexia case study and Dr. Whitaker carried out the linguistic analysis of the reading errors for the same case study. My interest in eye movements and their relationship to reading problems was inspired by the excellent work of Dr. Rayner. I have profited greatly from the many long hours of discussion with Dr. Whitaker, whose knowledge of the field of neuropsychology is unparalleled.

I am grateful also to the many friends who have encouraged me during the preparation of the manuscript including JEH, TCH, JHS, SD, and KBF. Lastly, I acknowledge the assistance and encouragement I have received from my wife, Priscilla, who has served as research assistant, secretary, and editor.

CONTENTS

LIST OF TABLES AND FIGURES

1 INTRODUCTION TO HUMAN NEUROPSYCHOLOGY

Reading and reading disabilities are areas of vital interest in neuropsychology. The number of researchers in the behavioral sciences who are involved in studies of reading disturbances has grown immensely over the past two decades. The progress made in understanding developmental dyslexia can be attributed to the clinical neurosciences. Although there has been a conspicuous failure to find a biological cause for reading disabilities, researchers continue to search for clues that eventually could reveal the brain dysfunction that is the causal mechanism in developmental dyslexia. This book will demonstrate that behavioral neurology and the newer science of neuropsychology are responsible, nonetheless, for significant contributions toward the goal of understanding the nature of dyslexia and the possible pathophysiology involved.

The neuropsychology of language has had an interesting and disputatious history during the last century. The French neurologist Pierre Paul Broca is generally recognized as the scientist who gave the first clinicopathological correlation for a language disorder. He discovered that a patient with an expressive or motor language disorder (presently known also as Broca's aphasia) had sustained damage to the foot of the inferior frontal gyrus--or third frontal convolution--in the left cerebral hemisphere. The apparent dissolution of this patient's expressive language capacity was quite complete. He could only utter the syllable "tan" and was thus nicknamed Tan Tan. Some critics argued--probably erroneously--that Tan Tan was, in fact, mentally defective before the brain injury. Despite this claim, Broca was credited with making the first definitive correlation between a higher mental function and a circumscribed brain region. Several years before Broca's discovery there were, of course, proponents of the localizationist notion. These phrenologists, among them Gall, Spurzheim, and Aubertin, argued that mental functions could be localized in specific brain regions. Little compelling evidence for their ideas was presented until Broca's discovery in 1861.

Pierre Marie (1906) was among the most vociferous of opponents to the view that lesions in the third frontal convolution (Broca's area) resulted in a syndrome of telegraphic speech, disturbed articulation, and agrammatism (Broca's aphasia). His most famous critique (with the pretentious title "The Third Frontal Convolution Plays No Special Role in Language") suggested that the lesion in Broca's patient far exceeded the boundaries of Broca's area in the inferior frontal region. Mohr (1976) has been a more recent critic of Broca's, presenting histological evidence that Broca's aphasia is caused by large lesions involving the operculum, insula, and subadjacent white matter. Once again, despite these opinions to the contrary, many neuroscientists are convinced that a relationship exists between expressive or Broca's aphasia and lesions in the inferior frontal gyrus.

The 26-year-old neurologist Carl Wernicke (1874) added clinicopathological correlations for two other aphasia syndromes at a time when many other scientists were replicating Broca's findings. He discovered that receptive aphasia, the language disorder characterized by a defect in phonemic hearing in the face of retained fluency, resulted from lesions in the posterior third of the first temporal gyrus of the left hemisphere. Although Wernicke was probably not the first to recognize the aphasia that bears his name (Wernicke's aphasia), he was the first to demonstrate a relationship between its clinical features and damage in the left temporal lobe.* Thus aphasia was no longer seen as a unitary neuropsychological syndrome with a single causal factor. A third aphasia, which Wernicke called Leitungsaphasie, was found to result from lesions in the connective fibers (the arcuate fasciculus) that run from Wernicke's area to Broca's area. The cardinal feature of this conduction aphasia is a repetition deficit, that is, the inability to repeat speech sounds that are heard, despite adequate speech comprehension and production. Three other syndromes of aphasia were described shortly after these discoveries: anomic aphasia, transcortical sensory aphasia, and transcortical motor aphasia. In each

---

*It should be noted that there is again general agreement that damage to Wernicke's region causes Wernicke's aphasia. One question that has arisen and that has been eloquently, if facetiously, asked by Bogen and Bogen (1976) is, "Where is Wernicke's region?" since there is so little agreement as to its exact anatomical locus.

of these syndromes there is a disorder of oral language that is characterized by linguistic disorders of speech production, comprehension, repetition, or naming.

Language expression can further be constrained by two other categories of disturbance. First, articulation difficulty can result from spastic or weak speech musculature. This slurring of speech (dysarthria) can be caused by lesions involving the fifth, seventh, ninth, tenth, or twelfth cranial nerves, the cerebellum (causing a scanning dysarthria), brain stem, basal ganglia, or corticobulbar tracts. Second, a patient may be unable to articulate because of a defect in the "motor memory" of speech sounds. Despite the fact that a patient may be able to spontaneously move his speech musculature, lick his lips, and put out his tongue, he has a special difficulty in performing these acts on command. This disorder, an apraxia of speech, is usually characterized by a problem in producing the beginning syllables of a word.

With regard to language comprehension, a special type of agnosia (a disorder of perceptual recognition) can occur that has a characteristic of aphasia. Patients with auditory verbal agnosia (pure word deafness) cannot understand speech but have normal expressive speech. These patients differ from Wernicke's aphasia in that they do not produce speech that is a string of meaningless, neologistic jargon but instead speak and read normally.

Consideration of language disturbances could not be complete, of course, if disorders of written language were not included. Clinicians have long noted the relationship between brain damage and reading disorders (see Benton and Joynt 1960). These disturbances were probably aphasic alexia, the reading dysfunction that is accompanied by defects in the speech and writing system. Charcot (1890) credited Gendrin with the clinical discovery of pure alexia, a disturbance of reading variously known in modern clinical neurology and neuropsychology as agnosic alexia or alexia without agraphia. Shortly after Broca's publication of the case of Tan Tan, numerous observations showed evidence of reading impairments in the absence of language disturbances (van der Abeele 1865; Broadbent 1872; Trousseau 1877; Kussmaul 1884).

Kussmaul gave the first extensive description of alexia, including it in his model of language disorders, but not until the observations of Dejerine (1891; 1892) was there any attempt to differentiate the alexias on the basis of clinical features or pathophysiology. The first syndrome described by Dejerine, now known as aphasic alexia, was characterized by alexia, agraphia, and paraphasia. The lesion responsible for this disorder was located in the left angular gyrus. The second syndrome, which was called pure word blindness, was characterized by a retained ability to write (both spontaneously and

FIGURE 1.1

Angular Gyrus

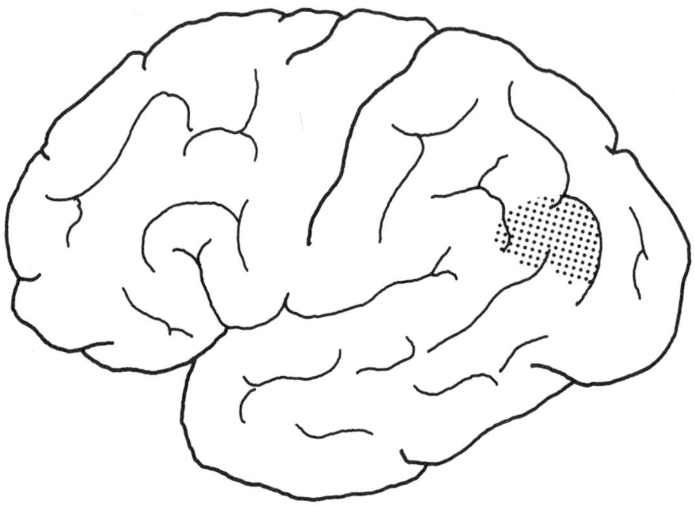

Source: Constructed by the author.

to dictation) but an inability to read. Presumably, lesions resulting in this syndrome interrupted the connections between the angular gyrus and the primary visual area. The alexic patient that Dejerine presented as an example of the syndrome of pure word blindness had a second lesion, this one in the splenium of the corpus callosum. The splenium is a mechanism for the interhemispheric transfer of information process in the left and right visual cortexes. The lesion then in the left visual association area prevented information from being transmitted to the "center for visual images of letters" in the left angular gyrus whereas the callosal lesion disconnected the right visual cortical areas from the left hemisphere. Although this explanation of the clinicopathological correlation in agnosic alexia (pure word blindness) is still the best available, Dejerine's ideas on this disconnection syndrome were not immediately accepted. Most notable of his critics were Wernicke (1903) and Marie (1906), neither of whom could accept the notion of a visual word center. Marie, not noted for being a shrinking violet in these matters, argued that it was ridiculous to speak of a visual word center because reading was a relatively new human acquisition and the brain could not have such a center for a function that only existed in a small minority of people and that appeared only fairly recently in human evolution! Nevertheless, Dejerine's observations and inferences as to the pathophysiological mechanisms in alexia have been supported by numerous investigators (see Geschwind 1965).

The foregoing discussion has shown that the left hemisphere plays a special role in language functions. Individuals who sustain damage to the lateral convexity of the left hemisphere usually lose some of their linguistic capacity, that is, if they are right-handed. Approximately 98 percent of right-handed individuals have language represented in the left hemisphere; some 68 percent of left-handed people also have language mechanisms in the left hemisphere; and the remaining minority defy description. Some of these people have language in the right hemisphere and some have it represented bilaterally.

Support for the notion that the left cerebral hemisphere governs verbal functions for most people comes from evidence other than the kind described in the previous remarks. The overwhelming amount of data on brain structure-mental function relationships came from studies of stroke patients up until the mid-twentieth century, although a good deal of data was collected after the World Wars (Goldstein 1948; Wepman 1951; Luria 1966; Newcombe 1969) from intensive studies of patients who had sustained penetrating missile wounds of the brain. A variety of methodological techniques are now used to determine the role of the left hemisphere in language functions. Electrical stimulation studies of epileptics who have undergone electrocorticography (stimulation mapping of the cortex) have provided strong evidence in favor of the superiority of the left hemisphere in language functions such as expression, comprehension, and naming. These studies--especially those of Penfield and Roberts (1958), Fedio and Van Buren (1974), and Ojemann and Whitaker (1978)--have served to show that the picture of language representation in the brain derived from lesion studies is very similar to that derived from stimulating the brain. Studies of the Wada technique (Wada 1949)--the introduction of sodium amytal into the carotid artery, which anesthetizes one hemisphere--provide further clear evidence that speech is lateralized in the left hemisphere in most people. The so-called split-brain operation studies of Sperry, Bogen, and Gazzaniga (see, for example, 1969) and their associates replicate this finding as well as give some compelling evidence that the right hemisphere also has a special function, that of visual-spatial relations. Laterality studies of normal subjects employing the visual-half field technique (White 1969; Pirozzolo 1977a), dichotic listening (Kimura 1966), and dichaptic shapes (Nebes 1974) point to these same relationships between the left hemisphere and language functions and the right hemisphere and spatial relations. Recently developed measures in regional cerebral blood flow (Ingvar and

Hagberg 1978) and electrophysiology (Molfese et al. 1975, 1978) contribute to the burgeoning field of laterality (or "hemisphericity") research.

Thus, the cerebral hemispheres, long thought to be mirror images of one another, have been found to be specialized for different psychological functions. These observations were remarkable, in part, because they were unprecedented discoveries in neurobiology; no other animal species appeared to have functional asymmetries. We now know, however, that many other animal species manifest asymmetries in psychological functions (see Harnad et al. 1977, for review). In addition, discoveries in the past decade have rejected the view that the hemispheres are mirror images of one another (Geschwind and Levitsky 1968). Anatomical asymmetries have been found in brain regions that are thought to be involved in the important functions of language comprehension and production (Galaburda et al. 1978). Geschwind and Levitsky observed that the left planum temporale (an auditory association region roughly corresponding to Wernicke's area) was larger than the right in most people studied. Wada et al. (1975) found a similar difference in size of the left over the right region corresponding to Broca's area. Fetal and neonatal brains have also been observed to have asymmetries in language zones (see, for example, Witelson and Pallie 1973). These results suggest that the larger size of these left hemisphere regions may provide a more favorable anatomical locus for language functions and that language may be genetically preprogrammed (or prewired) for the left hemisphere.

2 DEVELOPMENTAL DYSLEXIA

THE HISTORY AND NATURE OF CONGENITAL WORD BLINDNESS

Reports by Hinshelwood (1895) of brain-damaged adults who had lost the ability to read stimulated Pringle Morgan (1896) to describe a case of a 14-year-old boy with "congenital word blindness." This classic case study, which appeared in the British Medical Journal, was apparently the first published account of an otherwise normal child who had great difficulty learning to read and write. Reports from the child's teacher indicated that he was among the brightest in his school and that he had exceptional talents in other academic areas, such as mathematics (for example, he was able to carry out binomial expansions with relative ease). To account for this disability, Morgan suggested that the angular gyrus, the brain region suspected of being structurally altered in acquired dyslexia, was underdeveloped in this child. The notion of a maturational lag in the development of the area of the brain that subserves the reading process was thus conceived. Although this theory of the pathophysiology involved in reading disability has never received support from neuroanatomical, neurophysiological, or histochemical studies, it was reintroduced by Fisher (1910) and is still considered one of the most plausible explanations of the disorder (Geschwind 1965).

Several weeks before Morgan's paper appeared, the Royal Statistical Society awarded a medal to James Kerr, another British physician, for an essay that dealt in part with Kerr's observation that reading and writing difficulties occurred in children who curiously enough manifested no other cognitive disabilities. It appears that both Morgan and Kerr were unaware of the investigations undertaken by the other and both are generally credited with the clinical discovery

of developmental dyslexia. There are reports of reading disabilities in the German neurology literature that antedate the observations of Morgan and Kerr, but it is not clear as to whether these cases are examples of specific reading disabilities or more global cognitive deficiencies.

Within a few years, congenital word blindness was recognized as a clinical entity by numerous investigators, not only on the continent but elsewhere. Early contributions were made by Thomas (1905), Peters (1908), Hinshelwood (1917), Jackson (1906), McCready (1909-10), Orton (1925), and Thiele (1938).

Claiborne (1906) was among the first American clinicians to study the problem of congenital word blindness, but unfortunately his contribution was to have suggested that the disorder was endemic to English-speaking persons and that it was caused by the peculiarity and irregularity of the English phoneme-grapheme system. This assumption was, of course, almost immediately refuted because evidence had already been presented indicating that the disorder occurred in non-English-speaking children, especially Italian and Spanish disabled readers, and children whose use of non-alphabetic-phonetic writing systems (such as Japanese) would later be given as evidence against this explanation. Claiborne's position is, however, still shared by some modern clinicians and educators who have argued that using a more regular writing system such as the Initial Teaching Alphabet (which consists of symbols that have only one sound) should dramatically reduce the incidence of reading disability.

Researchers representing different fields of inquiry, such as psychology, linguistics, education, and the various disciplines of medicine (especially neurology and ophthalmology but also psychiatry and pediatrics), have been interested in the problem of reading disability. Surprisingly little communication between these disciplines took place and it gradually became clear that the syndrome would become one of the more controversial topics in scientific literature.

Numerous problems have plagued the study of reading disability, and the confusion that surrounds the issue exists, in part, because of the imprecise definition of the disorder. A myriad of other problems are readily apparent, among them the complexity of the term "reading," the lack of agreement as to the symptomatology of reading disability, the difficulties associated with specifying the condition as deviating from the normal, the number of terms used to describe reading problems (see Table 2.1), and the tremendous number of conflicting results that have been generated by studies of the cognitive deficits in these children (see Pirozzolo and Rayner 1978a).

Unfortunately, most of the research on dyslexia (or specific reading disability) has dealt with a rather nonspecific group of children who fail to read at the expected level. Some investigators, such as Sobotka and May (1977), for example, define dyslexia as a reading disability in which a child is six months behind grade level in reading. It is not surprising in view of this situation that estimates of the incidence of dyslexia in United States school children run as high as 10-15 percent and higher.

TABLE 2.1

Developmental Dyslexia Terminology

Congenital symbol amblyopia	Specific dyslexia
Congenital typholexia	Primary reading retardation
Congenital alexia	Backward reading
Amnesia visualis verbalis	Familial dyslexia
Congenital dyslexia	Familial congenital word blindness
Developmental alexia	Parietal dyslexia
Analfabetia partialio	Specific developmental dyslexia
Bradylexia	Perceptual handicapped
Strephosymbolia	Pure congenital visual aphasia
Specific reading disability	Learning disability
Constitutional dyslexia	

Source: Compiled by the author after Drew (1956).

Conversely, Rutter and Yule (1975) argued that distinctions must be made between children who are low achievers in reading (backward readers) and those who have a very specific reading retardation. It is notable that even the harshest critics of the concept of dyslexia (Rutter et al. 1970a and 1970b) would agree with the distinction between general reading backwardness and specific reading disability (dyslexia) on the basis of differences observed in speech and language ability and neurobehavioral development.

One of the most widely accepted definitions of developmental dyslexia was proposed in 1968 by the Research Group on Developmental Dyslexia of the World Federation of Neurology. According to this interdisciplinary group of experts representing neurology, pediatrics, psychology, and education, developmental dyslexia is "a disorder manifested by difficulty in learning to read despite conventional instruction, adequate intelligence and socio-cultural opportunity. It is dependent upon fundamental cognitive disabilities which are frequently of constitutional origin."

Kirk and Bateman (1962), McCarthy and McCarthy (1969), Doehring (1968), and Rourke (1976) suggested that disabled readers who survive this sort of elimination can be presumed to have a cerebral dysfunction to explain the reading deficit. It would appear that a neuropsychological approach in the search for a cerebral dysfunction is preeminent to discovering the nature of dyslexia. Most experts in the field would agree that "maturational lags" or "neurophysiological immaturity" (Bender 1959) are the most likely causal factors in dyslexia. Eisenberg (1966) delineated several factors that contribute to problems in reading acquisition. Among them are:

A. Extrinsic or social factors
    1. Quantitative and qualitative deficits in the teaching of reading and related skills
    2. Deficiencies in cognitive or intellectual stimulation
    3. Deficiencies in motivation associated with social pathology
B. Intrinsic or individual factors
    1. General mental deficiencies
    2. Sensory deficits
    3. Intellectual deficits
    4. Brain injuries
    5. Deficiencies in motivation associated with psychopathology
    6. Specific reading disability

That reading disability is related to social, psychiatric, sensory, or neurological handicaps is axiomatic. This book is concerned with a group of children for whom deficits in reading cannot be explained by sociocultural, psychopathological, sensory, motivational, or neuropathological reasons.

ETIOLOGY OF READING DIFFICULTIES

Quite apart from the foregoing, there are numerous investigators involved in research on reading who have demonstrated relationships between reading problems and other non-neuropsychological deficits. An abundance of literature, for example, can be found that links psychosexual and psychosocial problems with delayed reading acquisition. It is believed that the visual features of letters trigger fantasies that inhibit the reading process. Similarly, Blanchard (1946) suggested that retarded readers have a visual experience with letters that severely disrupts the reading process. It was suggested, for instance, that the letter "C" resembles an open mouth preparing to bite the disabled reader.

Buxbaum (1964) presented two case studies of reading retardation in which reading acquisition was delayed due to unresolved psychosexual conflicts. In a study of a large group of retarded readers, Kahn (1963) showed that good readers possess the characteristics of more healthy psychological functioning as viewed by the ego-analytic or neo-Freudian school of thought. In particular, Kahn suggested that reading achievement may depend upon adequate ego development typified by a high degree of self-discipline and the ability to postpone gratification. Other characteristics of good readers that seem to be lacking in disabled readers include high need for achievement and increased self-esteem as measured by projective personality tests (Pirozzolo 1973). Bender (1959) even suggested that there are strong similarities between schizophrenics and disabled readers. Both groups of children have poorly established ego boundaries and severe handicaps in understanding language symbols. Rabinovitch (1959) also pointed out that emotional factors are related to reading achievement.

The psychiatric implications associated with reading problems are quite clear, even if it is not clear as to whether a child with inadequate ego development does not learn to read readily because of emotional maladjustment or whether the disabled reader who is intelligent, sensitive, and competent in other areas of psychological functioning develops psychiatric symptoms as a result of a persistent failure in learning to read. In modern society a child who cannot read is at a severe disadvantage and his realization of this may result in an uncertainty about the world and about himself.

Recently evidence was presented that suggests a relationship between biochemical factors and reading disability. Feingold (1975) argued that children who suffer from various forms of minimal brain dysfunction (including reading disability and other learning and memory problems) have biochemical deficiencies that can be ameliorated with a proper diet, particularly one that minimizes the intake of artificial colorings and the like. There is, however, some evidence that the diet has no significant effect on variables such as hyperactivity and achievement in reading (Harley and Matthews 1976).

Menckes (1977) demonstrated a relationship between early infant bottle feeding and later learning difficulties. Previous research had revealed that infants whose blood tyrosive levels were higher than normal as a result of high-protein bottle feedings had a significantly higher incidence of perceptual and intellectual disabilities. The protein content of breast milk is considerably lower than that of formula milk. Menckes found that 13.8 percent of the children with learning disorders and 47.2 percent of the control children were breast-fed.

That genetic factors play an important role in reading difficulties is supported by a number of facts about the incidence of dyslexia. This discovery of the possible role of heredity in dyslexia was one of the first conclusive results to be shown by early research on the problem. Thomas (1905) studied two generations of a single family and found that six individuals suffered from reading disorders. Fisher (1905), Stephenson (1907), and Hinshelwood (1917) also made observations that tended to support the notion of a genetic etiology. Stephenson postulated that a recessive gene was responsible for the disorder on the basis of his study of three generations of a single family. The classic study, however, was carried out by Hallgren (1950) at the Stockholm Child Guidance Clinic. Of 276 consecutively evaluated dyslexics, Hallgren found that reading problems existed in 88 percent of the families of these children. On the basis of these results, Hallgren argued that developmental dyslexia follows a monohybrid autosomal dominant mode of inheritance.

Although genetic factors have been questioned by many investigators (Vernon 1957; Penn 1966), one further observation would indicate a relationship between genetic factors and reading disability. Most researchers have found that a disproportionate number of males are affected by dyslexia. There are some sources who found little or no sex bias (Vernon 1957; Jastak 1934) but the overwhelming amount of evidence would clearly show that males constitute the larger proportion of dyslexics. Our own analysis of these data indicates that the proportion of males in dyslexic groups is approximately four out of five.

Orton (1925, 1937) noted a relationship between children who had exceptional difficulty learning to read and write and adults who had sustained brain injuries. Clinical observations of these children indicated to Orton that a suspiciously high number of them were left-handed or had no lateral preference at all. Orton proposed that reading disability was due to the incomplete establishment of "cerebral dominance," that is, the two prominent symptoms (anomalies of handedness and reading problems) resulted from the congenital failure of one of the cerebral hemispheres to become the "dominant" or "major" control center for speech and language functions or for motor organization. Overzealous followers of Orton attempted to extend his theory into an elaborate conceptualization of the evolution of neurological organization in humans, which ontogenetically progressed from manifestations of amphibian-level neural organization (one of the first complex motor behaviors to appear in children is the amphibian-like homolateral crawling, which is the synchronous movement of the right arm and right leg as opposed to the later appearing heterolateral crawling, which is the synchronous movement of the right arm and the left leg) to manifestations of the highest levels of neural organization (the acquisition of speech and reading). These authors (for example, Delacato 1963) developed remedial programs that emphasized the importance of laterality to reading achievement. The program (which is still practiced at a small number of special facilities; see Krippner 1973) included encouraging the child to use only the right hand, sleeping in a specific position to increase lateral preference, refraining from listening to music since it interfered with the functioning of the language-dominant left hemisphere, and remedial work in reading and mathematics. An extensive study in the Chicago Public School System demonstrated that these treatments had no significant effect on achievement in reading or mathematics (Robbins 1968; Robbins and Glass 1969). Nevertheless, the notion that disabled readers suffer from incomplete cerebral dominance is widely held today, even if the terminology is misleading and many of Orton's theories of the neurological basis of learning and memory have been disproven.

MINIMAL BRAIN DYSFUNCTION, HYPERACTIVITY, AND RELATED PROBLEMS

Although the etiology and pathophysiology of developmental dyslexia are still very much in question, studies of a related problem, minimal brain dysfunction (MBD) are very close to providing conclusive evidence about the role of certain neurotransmitters in this disorder. MBD has been used as a catch-all term to describe any child who is apparently normal (that is, without confirmed neurological, sensory, motivational, or sociocultural deficiencies) and yet fails to learn or progress through developmental stages with his agemates. MBD has been conceptualized as including three kinds of children: those with pure learning disabilities (and without hyperkinesis), those with pure hyperkinesis (and without learning disabilities), and a mixed group. Most of the research to be discussed in this section concerns children with MBD who are in the second and third groups (hyperkinetic with and without learning disabilities).

The basic characteristics of children with MBD are:

Short attention span: This symptom is recognized in children when they cannot attend to a "still" activity, such as reading, for a long period of time. In a sense they are like children much younger than themselves in that they require fast-moving, high-interest activities to hold their attention.

Distractibility: This symptom is intimately related to the first. Children are unable to filter out "noise" from other sensory stimuli. In the auditory mode, nearby conversations will easily arouse the child's orienting reflex, and in the visual mode, any movement will distract the child from the task he is performing.

Impulsivity: This symptom, also seen in frontal lobe patients, is characterized by a "release from inhibition." Children cannot refrain from talking, taking wild guesses at answers, touching objects, and so on.

Poor motor integration: This symptom is part of a cluster of so-called soft signs that point to an organic brain syndrome. Clumsiness and dyscoordination in these children often cause great concern on the part of teachers and parents. Mirror movements, when children cannot move the fingers of one hand without moving the fingers of the other hand, and motor overflow, when children cannot move their eyes, for instance, without moving their heads also, are typical findings.

Hyperkinesis: There is no adequate description for the symptom of excessive, highly disorganized motor activity. It is, of course, the hallmark characteristic of minimal brain dysfunction and the symptom that gets the greatest amount of attention from researchers, teachers, and parents.

Most researchers are convinced that MBD has a biological cause and there is some fairly compelling evidence to support that view. Children with MBD show a paradoxical improvement after the administration of amphetamines and other stimulants (caffeine, methylphenidate [Ritalin], dextroamphetamine [Dexedrine], and so on). They experience a decrease in purposeless motor activity, an improvement in motor coordination, and an increase in their abilities to attend to school tasks. Amphetamines have the opposite effects on normals, that is, an increase in motor activity, distractibility, and impulsivity, and decreases in attention span and motor coordination. Numerous researchers in the neurosciences believe that these paradoxical effects after amphetamine administration indicate a neural basis for MBD. Few would suggest that focal brain damage is responsible. Lesions in the amygdala, hippocampus, globus pallidus, and septum have been found to result in hyperactivity in animals, but there is no evidence that any of these structures are "damaged" in children with MBD.

Pharmacological lesions in animals have also been observed to cause hyperactivity. There are numerous studies that purport to show an MBD analog with neonatal intracerebroventricular administration of 6-hydroxydopamine (6-OHDA), which depletes two neurotransmitters, dopamine and norepinephrine. Several other animal

MBD models have been developed that emphasize the importance of these two neurotransmitters in the etiology of MBD. Most of these studies have used rats; there is good generalizability from rats to humans in these studies because human adrenergic central nervous system pathways are very similar to rats'. In addition, there are other indications that these MBD models have validity when the pathophysiology of similar disorders is considered.

Some interesting similarities arise in the study of other movement disorders. About 25 years ago, the neuropharmacological agent reserpine was first used to treat psychoses. Very little was known about the antipsychotic action of reserpine, but it was observed that many patients taking the drug had a rigidity and hypokinesis (decreased motor activity) similar to that found in persons with Parkinson's disease. Parkinson's disease is a disorder marked by a very coarse tremor and difficulty initiating voluntary movements. Several years later, the Swedish pharmacologist Arvid Carlsson showed that the neostriatum (the caudate and putamen) contained large amounts of dopamine and that administration of reserpine depleted dopamine. Carlsson speculated that dopamine was important in the control of movement by the extrapyramidal motor system. Histological studies later followed that showed that dopamine was indeed depleted in the neostriatum of Parkinson's patients. As treatment for Parkinson's disease a precursor of dopamine, L-dopa, was developed (because dopamine does not cross the blood-brain barrier). A little over a decade ago, enough evidence had been collected to show that L-dopa could ameliorate the effects of Parkinson's disease that it became the treatment of choice in the extrapyramidal disorder.

Another extrapyramidal disorder, Huntington's chorea, has the clinically opposite symptoms, that is, hyperkinesis with large undershooting and overshooting of voluntary movements. Just as there seems to be neuronal loss in the posterioventral group (globus pallidus and substantia nigra) and dopamine depletion in the neostriatum of Parkinson's, Huntington's patients seem to have neuronal loss in the anteriodorsal group, the neostriatum, and an increase in dopamine but a decrease in acetylcholine in the caudate and putamen.

It is not surprising that some of the early researchers of the preadolescent hyperkinesis syndrome called it a "choreic syndrome" (Prechtl and Stemmer 1958). In addition to the evidence of paradoxical response to amphetamines, there is some further support for the theory that there is a biochemical basis for MBD and that it may not be dissimilar to the mechanisms involved in other movements disorders. Evidence for the role of dopaminergic mechanisms in the etiology of MBD comes from the pandemic of von Economo's encephalitis early in the twentieth century. In adults, this variety of encephalitis resulted in parkinsonian symptoms (hypokinesis and resting tremor), which were believed to be associated with basal ganglia destruction. Children affected by von Economo's encephalitis, on the other hand, did not present with parkinsonian symptoms but with symptoms of MBD (hyperkinesis, short attention span, and so on). Along with other evidence, this observation would suggest a basic difference in the balance of neurotransmitters in the extrapyramidal systems of children and adults. Clinical trials with MBD children have shown antiparkinsonian drugs to be useful in treating hyperkinesis, just as they are useful in the treatment of hypokinesis in Parkinson's disease (Jackson and Pelton, 1978).

Wender was among the first to suggest that there is a biochemical basis for the MBD syndrome and that it may be related to the monoamine neurotransmitters. As mentioned previously, there is some evidence for this because many hyperkinetic children respond dramatically to treatment with stimulant drugs, which are known to interact with monoamine neurotransmitters. A controversy exists, however, over the exact mechanism of action of these drugs in MBD children. Wender hypothesized that MBD children have functionally underactive norepinephrine systems, whereas other investigators proposed that the beneficial effects of amphetamines are principally due to an increase in the availability of dopamine at certain central nervous system receptor sites. Data on the distribution of neurotransmitters in the brains of MBD children is understandably difficult to obtain. The best direct evidence of the role of the monoamines in MBD children comes from studies of monoamine metabolites in the cerebrospinal fluid of these children (Shetty and Chase 1976). Other evidence employs animal models of MBD, examples of which will be discussed below.

Alpern and Greer (1977) demonstrated a dopaminergic basis for the effects of amphetamine using a mouse hyperkinetic model. They used 30-day-old mice to show that amphetamine prolonged the latency to flurothyl-induced myoclonus (operationally defined as the first jerk of the head or neck musculature after inhalation of flurothyl), which is thought to be a measure of hypokinesis. In another study, they sought to determine whether catecholamines could simulate the effects of amphetamine (because amphetamine is known to facilitate catecholinergic transmission by increasing release and blocking the reuptake of dopamine and norepinephrine). The dopaminergic agonist, apomorphine, and the noradrenergic agonist, clonidine, were both used in this experiment. Apomorphine decreased myoclonic susceptibility whereas clonidine increased susceptibility, thus indicating that amphetamine may attenuate neural excitability in the MBD syndrome.

Brase and Loh (1978), however, argued that there may be a relationship between serotonin and MBD. Weanling rats, for instance, become hyperactive when they are given an L-tryptophan- (similar in chemical structure to serotonin) free diet for about two weeks. While this observation is interesting, it gives no clues to the mechanisms in human MBD, although two other observations certainly provide some suggestive evidence. Blood serotonin concentrations in MBD children are characteristically lower than those of normals. Further, in a study of children whose blood serotonin levels increased to normal during a period of hospitalization, marked improvement was seen in the clinical symptoms of MBD. How amphetamine interacts with serotonin systems is fairly well known. It is not known whether the decrease in blood serotonin is due to the L-tryptophan deficiency or whether it is paralleled by a deficiency of serotonin in vivo. Rutledge and his colleagues (1977) showed that amphetamine releases serotonin in vitro from various rat brain regions and other studies have shown that serotonin-depleting agents enhance locomotor response to amphetamine.

Jeri Sechzer and her colleagues (1977) developed an animal model of MBD in neonatal kittens. They produced the symptom complex of MBD--including decreased learning ability, hyperactivity, and impulsivity--with mid-saggital sections of the corpus callosum, the large commissural tract carrying fibers from homologous regions of one hemisphere to the other. After the surgeries, the split-brain kittens' open field activity was increased (in relation to controls), their ability to learn visual discrimination tasks was decreased, and the time they spent with test objects (used as a measure of impulsivity) was decreased. Neonatal split-brain kittens took longer to learn the experimental tasks than normals but, interestingly, those split-brain kittens who were given amphetamine learned the tasks more rapidly than normals. The other measures showed similar relationships. Other investigators observing the behavioral deficits in MBD children argued that it may be a consequence of deficient transmission across the corpus callosum (Beaumont 1976). These observations would bring up the question of the role of the corpus callosum in humans. Early neuroanatomists thought it merely performed a mechanical function, that is, it kept the cerebral hemispheres from sagging. Neurosurgeons only half-facetiously thought that it served only to permit the spread of electrical discharges during epileptic seizures from one hemisphere to the other. When the aforementioned observations are analyzed with other evidence of the role of the corpus callosum, it may be suggested that the callosum is a central programming device that, when sectioned, isolates the neuronal processes of the two hemispheres from each other and limits the interplay of excitatory and inhibitory processes. Sechzer and her colleagues suggest that the amphetamine that ameliorates the MBD symptoms facilitates the release of norepinephrine in the CNS and increases synaptic transmission, a very plausible argument in view of other evidence from animal studies.

Another interesting piece of evidence to support this notion would appear to come from the studies of anatomical maturation in the human brain undertaken by Yakovlev and Lecours (1967). These investigators found that the corpus callosum is one of the last regions to reach anatomical maturity as measured by the relative completion of the myelination process. It very well could be that delayed myelination of the corpus callosum is responsible for the MBD syndrome (just as the late myelination of the angular gyrus has been suggested as the causal mechanism in developmental dyslexia) and that the paradoxical effects of amphetamine are explained by one of the previously discussed mechanisms of action. Additional evidence is certainly needed to determine the relative contribution of each of the systems mentioned. Contrary to popular claims, however, the lack of specificity of the amphetamine treatment program for certain children with MBD, which helps them to learn and control unwanted involuntary movements, is no argument against its use.

EVIDENCE FOR SUBGROUPS OF DYSLEXIA

A serious problem in the treatment of developmental dyslexia has been the assumption that it is a single, homogenous clinical entity with a specific profile of higher cortical dysfunctions and that there is a single causative factor underlying the disorder. During the last decade, evidence has been collected that implies that these assumptions are probably false. The following review strongly suggests that two subgroups of dyslexia have been isolated from large clinical populations by a differential diagnosis of the cognitive deficits in these children.

The attempt to describe subtypes of developmental dyslexia derives from an early emphasis on the diagnosis and remediation of reading problems, perhaps best exemplified by the work of Wepman (1960, 1962, 1964, 1965), Myklebust (1965), and Boder (1971, 1973). Other attempts to make systematic neuropsychological analyses not specifically aimed at educational remediation but rather at demonstrating that the developmental dyslexias can be divided into independent neuropsychological syndromes have been made by Kinsbourne and Warrington (1963), Mattis et al. (1975), Denckla and Rudel (1974, 1976), Rudel and Denckla (1974), Pirozzolo and Hess (1976), and Pirozzolo (1977b).

Wepman (1965) proposed the "modality concept" to illustrate the principle that even normal development is characterized by manifestations of the asynchronous development of visual and auditory skills. Reading acquisition requires both visual and auditory abilities, and the neural substrates that are related to the performance of these skills develop at different rates even in the normal child. The rate of development of neural differentiation is governed by genetic predisposition as well as external stimulation. Wepman suggested that these perceptual modalities do not reach a stage of equalization of function until around age nine in the normal child, whereas Myklebust and Johnson (1962) argued that this asynchrony may be more pronounced and may persist beyond the age of nine in the disabled reader. Based on results of tests in a language battery, Myklebust (1965) concluded that dyslexia is indeed characterized by either auditory or visual symptomatology. Quiros (1964) also found auditory and visual subtypes of dyslexia using linguistic measures.

Boder (1971, 1973) examined reading and spelling samples of 107 dyslexic subjects and identified two patterns of performance among these children. One group of dyslexics (dysphonetic) exhibited weaknesses in auditory skills and read words as visual gestalts rather than decoding them into phonetic units. Spelling errors were typified by the misapplication of phoneme-to-grapheme rules. Because these children attempt to bypass phonology whenever possible, they also made reading and spelling errors that involved semantic substitutions. There have been attempts to explain this phenomenon of semantic paralexia in acquired dyslexics (Saffran et al. 1976), callosal patients (Brown 1972), and in developmental dyslexics (Pirozzolo and Rayner 1979), and it is possible that reading in these patients may depend upon the right hemisphere's ability to abstract meaning directly from the visual features of text.

According to Boder, a second group of dyslexics (dyseidetic) exhibit weaknesses in the ability to discriminate and analyze the visual gestalts of words. Although phonetic abilities are intact in these children, reading suffers from the laborious process of sounding out even the most familiar combination of letters. Spelling errors frequently involve letter and word reversals and confusions. In contrast to dysphonetic dyslexics, dyseidetics appear to spell everything phonetically because of an inability to revisualize the correct word. A third group of dyslexics was also identified by Boder--a mixed dysphonetic-dyseidetic group. It is unclear as to whether this group represents a single dyslexia syndrome and it is doubtful that clues to mechanisms related to reading disability will be revealed by studies concerned with this group of children since they remain, as Boder points out, virtually "alexic" through high school age and are the most severely handicapped educationally.

Kinsbourne and Warrington (1963) compared two groups of disabled readers who had WISC verbal-performance IQ discrepancies of 20 points or more in either direction. Consistent with other results they found that the two groups had different patterns of associated difficulties: the children with lower verbal IQs showed clinical signs of impaired language expression and reception whereas the children with lower performance IQs showed intact language but impaired finger differentiation, greater disability in mathematics, visuoconstructive defects, and left-right disorientation. These results suggest that at least two groups of dyslexics can be identified on the basis of neuropsychological test performance: one a language disorder and the other a developmental Gerstmann syndrome. The former group is characterized by a lower verbal IQ, late onset of language, and phonetically inappropriate spelling errors. These symptoms are clinically indicative of a mild but generalized language disorder. The latter group has neuropsychological symptoms that closely resemble those in a group of brain-damaged adults who have the tetrad of symptoms constituting Gerstmann's syndrome: finger agnosia, dyscalculia, directional disorientation, and dysgraphia (Benson and Geschwind 1970; Kinsbourne and Warrington 1965; Pirozzolo and Rayner 1978b). As expected, these children make an inordinate number of spelling errors that involve letter confusions and reversals.

The final and perhaps most striking sets of observations were based on clinical neuropsychological evaluations of large numbers of dyslexic children and adults (Mattis et al. 1975; Pirozzolo and Hess 1976; Denckla and Rudel 1976). The general finding among these studies is in agreement with Critchley (1970) that one group of dyslexics has severe language disabilities that suggest an "aphasiological" disorder. Denckla and Rudel (1976) demonstrated that these children are deficient in the ability to carry out rapid verbal tasks. Similarly, Mattis et al. noted that anomia is often the most prominent presenting feature in this form of dyslexia. Pirozzolo et al. (1977), in a neurolinguistic analysis of the reading and writing of a dyslexic with the aforementioned symptoms of a language disorder or auditory-linguistic dyslexia, demonstrated agrammatism, probably the first such observation in a case of developmental dyslexia.

The second group of dyslexics have been shown to have weaknesses in visual perceptual (Mattis et al. 1975), spatial, and oculomotor (Pirozzolo and Rayner 1978b) functions. Finger agnosia, directional disorientation, and atypical handwriting orientations have also been observed in children with this form of dyslexia.

Mattis et al. (1975), in a study of 252 developmental and acquired dyslexics, concluded on the basis of their neuropsychological test results that there were no significant differences between the groups of developmental and acquired dyslexics in terms of the nature or severity of higher cortical dysfunctions, thus suggesting that developmental dyslexia is not behaviorally distinguishable from acquired dyslexia. It is often reported that virtually every disorder of higher cortical function can be found with greater frequency in groups of dyslexic children than in control groups (Satz and van Nostrand 1973) and this is often marshalled as evidence that dyslexia is a language problem caused by a nonspecific minimal brain dysfunction. The evidence reported here does not support this claim. The literature reviewed strongly suggests that two subgroups of developmental dyslexia exist and that they can be differentiated on the basis of neuropsychological tests. In this book, the two groups will be referred to as auditory-linguistic dyslexics and visual-spatial dyslexics. The auditory-linguistic group is characterized by deficits in verbal-learning ability and is roughly similar to the dysphonetic dyslexics described by Boder (1971) and the language disorder dyslexics described by Kinsbourne and Warrington (1963) and by Mattis et al. (1975). Evidence suggests that this disorder occurs at least four to five times more frequently than the visual-spatial form of dyslexia (Boder 1971). The visual-spatial group is characterized by deficits in visual perceptual ability and is roughly similar to the dyseidetic dyslexics described by Boder, the developmental Gerstmann group described by Kinsbourne and Warrington (1963), and the visual perceptual dyslexics described by Mattis et al. (1975).

The objective of the research described in Chapter 4 is to present evidence in favor of these two typologies of dyslexia by demonstrating that their performance on experimental measures of visual information-processing abilities differs. Specifically, these two subgroups of dyslexics will be compared with each other and with normal readers on (1) a lateralized visual perceptual task, (2) an eye movement latency task, and (3) eye movement patterns during reading. In the next four sections of this chapter, previous studies and findings regarding each of these tasks will be discussed.

DYSLEXIA AND LATERAL ASYMMETRIES IN VISUAL PERCEPTION

Mishkin and Forgays (1952) were the first to tachistoscopically present words to the right and left of a fixation point, and they found that words were recognized more easily when they were exposed in the right visual field. Many other researchers have produced these same laterality effects and, when the experiment is properly controlled under the conditions noted by White (1969), the results favor the following explanation. When words are presented for intervals of less than 100 milliseconds (which does not allow sufficient time for an eye movement), recognition is superior in the right visual field because of its direct contralateral connections with the language mechanisms of the left hemisphere. Words presented to the left visual field are not recognized with the same degree of accuracy, presumably because there is a temporal lag in the time necessary for the information to cross the corpus callosum to reach the language-dominant hemisphere (Kimura 1961). Although words are typically better identified by normal adults and children in the right visual field, certain visuospatial stimuli are better identified in the left visual field because the right hemisphere is superior in carrying out nonverbal, visuospatial analyses. Left visual field advantages have been achieved for such visuospatial stimuli as faces (Pirozzolo and Rayner 1979), dots (Kimura 1966), and the perception of line orientation (Fontenot and Benton 1972), and these remain fairly stable under the proper conditions (compare with Pirozzolo 1977b).

Although disabled readers do show a left visual field superiority in face recognition (Marcel and Rajan 1975; Pirozzolo and Rayner 1979), they do not show the same right visual field superiority for word recognition (Marcel et al. 1974). In the study reported by Marcel et al. (1974), poor readers showed no recognition asymmetry, and it was argued that the right hemispheres of poor readers are superior to those of normal readers in processing linguistic information. In a more recent study of gifted, normal, and disabled readers, Kerschner (1977) demonstrated that gifted readers show a greater right visual field superiority than normal readers whereas disabled readers show no asymmetry at all. This suggests that the degree of lateralization of language functions may indeed be related to linguistic ability. These studies appear to support Orton's theory (1937) that incomplete cerebral dominance for language is responsible for the reading deficit. Invoking the principle of incomplete cerebral dominance is perhaps anachronistic and adds little to the understanding of the disorder. The term has been used to suggest that (1) there is bilateral representation of language function and that the hemispheres compete for expression, (2) the classical language areas, probably including Broca's area, Wernicke's area, and the angular gyrus, do not sufficiently support language functions, and (3) that the fiber pathways interconnecting the left hemisphere language mechanisms are not fully established or space-committed, thus implying a neurophysiological immaturity.

In contrast to the results achieved by Marcel et al. (1974), Yeni-Komshian et al. (1975) reported that poor readers have a larger right visual field superiority than good readers. This would suggest that poor readers are not less lateralized for language functions but rather are more lateralized. Reading disability may therefore be related to a cerebral dysfunction in the right hemisphere or by a callosal syndrome that degrades the transmission of information from the right to the left hemisphere. Although there is very little evidence to support a right hemisphere deficit in dyslexia, these results may be explained by differences in the deficits presented by the dyslexics in this study. Further attention to this problem is given in Chapter 4.

Witelson (1977) suggested that dyslexics did not show a right visual field superiority in her visual half-field study due to a bilateral neural involvement in visuospatial processing. Clearly, there are neurons in both hemispheres that are involved in visuospatial information processing, but Witelson's hypothesis is probably meant to imply that bilateral representation of spatial functions somehow interferes with the establishment of language function.

In a recent study, Pirozzolo and Rayner (1979) used only dyslexics who had undergone neuropsychological evaluations and could be said to have an auditory-linguistic form of dyslexia. These disabled readers showed no right visual field superiority for words, although they had normal left field advantages for a nonverbal task (facial recognition). Pirozzolo and Rayner (1979) suggested that these results imply that auditory-linguistic dyslexics suffer from the pathologically slow transmission of linguistic information within the left hemisphere whereas visuospatial information processing is normally executed in the right hemisphere. This evidence, along with the fact that there are no neurophysiological or electrophysiological data showing that disabled readers have anomalous lateralization, that is, language is not represented in the left hemisphere, suggests that auditory-linguistic dyslexia strongly resembles an aphasiological disorder.

Bouma and Legein (1977) used a modification of the hemifield paradigm in a study of foveal and parafoveal word recognition. They presented letters and words to dyslexic and normal readers in central vision and displaced by one degree. Results indicated that there were no differences in foveal letter recognition, although parafoveal letter recognition was lower in dyslexics. Bouma and Legein suggested that dyslexic subjects have a useful visual field that is narrower than the functional visual field of good readers.

In the visual hemifield study that will be reported here, an analysis of the neurobehavioral profiles of each of the groups might predict the following results:

Normal readers will show a right visual field superiority for word recognition, reflecting the specialization of the left hemisphere in linguistic functions. These laterality effects should be constant at both one and two degrees of visual angle.

Auditory-linguistic dyslexics will show no visual field superiority for word recognition, reflecting the depressed ability of the left hemisphere to process linguistic information. Differences between normals and auditory dyslexics in foveal word recognition are not expected and it is not expected that differences in the left visual field performance between the groups will be observed, thus suggesting no increase in linguistic capacity of the right hemisphere in auditory-linguistic dyslexics.

Visual-spatial dyslexics will show a right visual field superiority for word recognition and a more pronounced decrease in parafoveal word recognition than the other experimental groups. As suggested by Bouma and Legein (1977), this may reflect a constricted visual field. No differences should be observed between visual-spatial dyslexics and either auditory-linguistic dyslexics or normals in foveal word recognition.

READING RESEARCH, PERCEPTUAL SPAN, AND VISUAL FUNCTION IN READING

Toward the end of the nineteenth century many important contributions to the understanding of the reading process were made by experimental psychologists. Working in Wundt's laboratory for experimental psychology, Cattell (1885, 1886) was able to determine some characteristics of the word recognition process. Huey's text (1908), The Psychology and Pedagogy of Reading, surveyed the great progress made in the field up until that time and remains a remarkably accurate characterization of the basic processes in reading. Similarly, Woodworth's classic monograph Experimental Psychology (1938) is widely recognized as a germinal contribution to the study of skilled reading.

Sometime between the publication of Huey's volume and the appearance of Woodworth's, reading research became less the province of experimental psychology (possibly due to the influence of Watson and the popular transition to behaviorism) and had taken on a more applied character. Researchers in education began doing the most significant proportion of research and their interests seemed to be centered on the improvement of reading ability.

One of the most important issues in reading research is the identification of the amount of visual information useful to the skilled reader during a single fixation. A reader is able to apprehend only a small amount of information during a single fixation. Woodworth (1938) noted that the reader is able to recognize words in the vertical plane from as far away as two to three lines above and below fixation. In addition, the reader is able to recognize words that are a short distance to the right and left of fixation. Quite obviously, it is this horizontal span of apprehension that is useful to the reader. Specifying the nature and extent of this span has been a very controversial topic, and the use of different methods to determine the amount of information acquired during a single fixation has resulted in rather conflicting results (reviewed by Rayner 1975). One method of estimating the perceptual span used by numerous researchers (Taylor 1965; Rubino and Minden 1973) is the method of dividing the number of fixations into the number of characters appearing on a line or in a passage of text. Hochberg (1970), among others, argued against this parsimonious explanation of the perceptual span because it assumes that there is no overlap or irregularity in the spans.

A second method of estimating the perceptual span involves brief tachistoscopic exposures of letters and words. Sperling (1960) pointed out, however, that this estimate does not correspond to the perceptual span because a reader can perceive a great amount of information, part of which is sometimes lost when subjects are asked to report the letters or words presented in a tachistoscope.

A third method, described by Huey (1908), involves the fixation of a point and the identification of stimuli, which are then displaced by various distances from the fixation. Using this method, Bouma (1973) found that subjects can only report four or five letters around the fixation point and that there is significantly better recognition in the right visual field (see, for example, Bouma and Legein 1977).

A fourth method involves providing the subject with a fixed span (or window) of information that can be manipulated. The limits of the perceptual span are presumably reached when smaller windows that are disruptive to the reader are increased until the reader's eye movements and comprehension are optimized.

Rayner and McConkie (see, for example, Rayner and McConkie 1976; Rayner 1978b) have developed a more sophisticated system for determining the perceptual span while readers are actually engaged in reading text. By using a computer-based display system that makes various changes in words on a cathode ray tube (CRT) at some point in the process and monitoring the eye movements of the subjects, these investigators closely approached an accurate depiction of the perceptual span. Their results suggest that skilled readers obtain semantic information from only a small area around the fixation, that they acquire letter and word shape information from an area as large as 17 to 19 character spaces, and that there is a significant asymmetry of the perceptual span such that information is acquired from further to the right of fixation than the left.

Research on the perceptual span during reading and other visual sensory and perceptual factors is pertinent here because of numerous suggestions that disabled readers have constricted visual fields and that they are characterized by a number of other visual handicaps. Eames found that disabled readers differ from normal readers in that they have a lower median amplitude of fusion convergence (1934), that they have a higher incidence of incoordination of the eyes and farsightedness (1935), and that they have constricted visual fields (1936). In the latter study, Eames suggested that restricted visual fields are causally related to learning problems and reading difficulties in particular. He revealed the visual field defects by campometric examinations in the four principal diameters (horizontal, vertical, oblique 1, and oblique 2). Blake and Dearborn (1935) found a higher percentage of disabled readers to have farsighted astigmatism than good readers. Recently, Frank and Levinson (1976) suggested that dyslexics have lower "blurring speeds" than good readers and that this cerebellar-vestibular symptom may adversely affect the reading process by reducing clear vision and making proper orientation difficult.

Contrary to the results noted above, the overwhelming proportion of studies of visual function in reading disability have indicated that visual defects are unrelated to reading disability. In an early challenge to Eames's work, Witty (1936) concluded that poor readers are not characterized by a higher incidence of visual defects such as deficient acuity, fusion, or muscle balance. In the same year, Swanson and Tiffin (1936) also found visual sensory and perceptual deficits to be unrelated to reading disability. Vernon (1957) concluded that there was no evidence to suggest visual perceptual disorders in disabled readers from performance on picture recognition, facial recognition, and other visuospatial tasks. Gruber (1962) found no correlation between binocular coordination and reading disability. In a recent paper, another aspect of visuospatial ability, oculomotor scanning, was studied and it was concluded that the simple oculomotor skill necessary for reading is overlearned by the time children learn to read. Variation in reading ability, therefore, cannot be accounted for by oculomotor factors (Stennett et al. 1972-73). Spache (1976) also stated that beginning readers have a fundamental oculomotor skill that is well developed and there is no developmental trend toward improvement in this ability. Together these studies would suggest that visuospatial sensory and perceptual skills (including oculomotor scanning) are not related to the syndrome of developmental dyslexia.

DYSLEXIA AND SACCADIC EYE MOVEMENT REACTION TIMES

Several studies of the latencies for oculomotor reaction have recently been carried out. These studies are concerned with the amount of time required to initiate a saccadic eye movement to a simple visual target such as a vertical bar of light, a dot, or a word. Studies of normal saccadic eye movement reaction time to nonverbal targets (Westheimer 1954; Bartz 1962; White et al. 1962; Robinson et al. 1976; Baloh and Honrubia 1976) have uncovered latency values in the range of 160-200 milliseconds. These measurements have been based on both randomly and nonrandomly presented signals but have generally tended to deal with saccadic amplitudes that are much larger than those normally made in reading.

Studies employing words as targets and requiring saccades that are roughly the amplitude of those made in reading have been reported by Rayner (1978a). Interestingly, reaction time to targets to the right of fixation was significantly shorter than reaction time to the left. Lesevre (1964, 1966, 1968) also demonstrated this reaction time asymmetry although, in a similar study, Dossetor and Papaioannou (1975) reported an asymmetry in oculomotor reaction time but one that is shorter for saccades going to the left. In this experiment, however, targets appeared 40 degrees to the right and left of fixation, distances clearly not within the range of saccades made during reading.

Certain other observations have been made concerning saccadic eye movement latencies that warrant consideration in the analysis of the dyslexias. Studies of normal and disabled readers conducted by Lesevre (1964, 1966, 1968) have revealed that, whereas normal readers have shorter saccadic latencies to the right, disabled readers show no such asymmetry. Lesevre considered the absence of gaze lateralization to be symptomatic of a disorder in processing visuospatial information that characterizes some disabled readers. Dossetor and Papaioannou (1975), on the other hand, found quite a different pattern of asymmetry in a study of dyslexic and normal readers. Reaction times for dyslexics were shorter for movements to the right whereas normal children and adults showed shorter reaction times to the left. The reaction times reported for their subjects, however, were significantly longer than those reported by any of the aforementioned investigators. Mean reaction times for dyslexics was over 500 milliseconds whereas normals averaged over 400 milliseconds. Cohen and Ross (1977) found that there were no differences for saccadic latencies to the right and left for either good or poor readers in their study of the effects of warning intervals and target eccentricities on saccadic latencies in disabled and normal readers but found that disabled readers were deficient in the ability to maintain a fixation prior to the onset of a target.

In the study to be reported we should expect no differences between the performance of auditory-linguistic dyslexics and normal readers in saccadic eye movement reaction times. Specifically, both groups will be expected to show a shorter latency for initiating movement to the right whereas the visual-spatial dyslexic group may show a faster reaction time to signals appearing in the left visual field. The asymmetry for normals and auditory-linguistic dyslexics is thought to be associated with the superior motor organization in the left hemisphere of most right-handers. There is some evidence (Rayner and Pirozzolo 1978) that is suggestive of this relationship since it has been demonstrated that left-handed groups do not show lateral asymmetries for saccadic latencies. It is suggested that normals and auditory-linguistic dyslexics have shorter saccadic latencies to stimuli appearing in the right visual field because visuomotor processing is more efficiently performed by these groups as compared to the visual-spatial dyslexics. When stimuli are projected into the right visual field, the visual cortex of the left hemisphere receives and begins the processing of this information before the right hemisphere. Rightward saccades are generated by parietal association and premotor association mechanisms in the left hemisphere, and this pathway is presumed to be intact in normals and auditory-linguistic dyslexics. The possible pathophysiology in visual-spatial dyslexia suggested by Morgan (1896), Fisher (1910), Geschwind (1965), and others is the late maturation of the visual association areas, especially of the left hemisphere. It is expected, then, that visual-spatial dyslexics will have increased visuomotor reaction times, especially for rightward movements, since processing in these pathways is presumed to be less efficient than in normals.

The neuroanatomic localization of the pathophysiology in auditory-linguistic is almost certainly within the left (language-dominant) hemisphere. Focal cerebral dysfunctions are probably not the causal factors in dyslexia but rather are maturational lags in the development of regions of the brain that subserve the reading process. The regions which are implicated include the left cortical visual association areas and their connections with the frontal motor and premotor areas for visual-spatial dyslexia and the auditory association areas of the left hemisphere and their subcortical connections with the frontal motor and premotor areas.

DYSLEXIA AND THE ROLE OF EYE MOVEMENTS IN READING

Javal was probably the first visual scientist to observe that during reading the eyes make a series of very rapid, jerky movements across a line of text. Until Javal's discovery around 1879, it was assumed that the eyes moved continuously from left to right along the horizontal plane of the text. Several years later, Dearborn suggested that the eye "tends to follow each shift of attention in order to bring the object nearer the fovea." Simply stated, this is the role of eye movements in reading--to bring visual information that is located in the periphery into the region of clearest vision so that the brain can carry out further higher level cognitive operations that will translate the visual information into meaning.

There are three principal components of eye movements during reading: saccadic eye movements, fixations, and regressions (see Rayner 1978a). Fixations constitute about 90 percent of total reading time and the remaining 10 percent is used for saccadic eye movements. The average length of a saccade is approximately two degrees or about eight character spaces although great variability is evident in this aspect of eye behavior during reading.

Fixations average about 250 milliseconds in duration and the average time to move the eyes from fixation to fixation is around 35 milliseconds. Fixation duration varies with reader ability, difficulty of text, and reading speed but the time that it takes to move the eyes is much more constant and independent of the aforementioned factors. It is generally assumed that most of the information acquired during a fixation is transmitted to the cortex during the fixation whereas little or no information is transmitted during the saccadic movement due to partial visual suppression (Matin 1974).

Regressions are the final component of reading eye movements to be considered. These right-to-left movements constitute about 15 percent of the total number of saccades made by adult readers. Buswell (1922) was one of the first psychologists to study these eye movement phenomena in a study of the developmental changes in reading rates. He demonstrated that beginning readers make approximately three times as many fixations per line of print (18.6), 10 times as many regressions per line of print (5.1), and had fixation durations that were 2.5 times as long as that of college readers (600 milliseconds). Similarly, Taylor (1965) showed that first grade readers make regressive movements equal to about 25 percent of the total number of saccades whereas college students make regressions at the rate of 15 percent of the total number of saccades. These observations suggest that when reading proficiency is attained both regression frequency and fixation durations decrease.

The relationship between reading ability and regression frequency is not a simple one, however. Regressions can be a function of unfamiliar text (as Buswell has indicated in an account of adults reading eye movements using foreign language grammar texts), a neurological disorder affecting oculomotor control (Hartje 1972), and reading problems associated with a visual-spatial form of dyslexia (Pirozzolo and Rayner 1978b).

Although the preceding remarks provide some normative account of reading eye movement patterns, they ignore the very important question concerning eye behavior: what determines where the eye is sent during a saccade? There is perhaps a tacit assumption in the previous discussion (as there was for almost a century in reading research) that the eye moves some random distance (possibly determined by reading habits of the individual reader) and stops at regular intervals that are independent of the visual, syntactic, and semantic features of the text. This is probably not the case. Rayner and McConkie (1976) proposed five classes of eye guidance models: minimal control models, low-level control models, high-level control models, process-monitoring control models, and mixed models of eye control. Minimal control models suggest that the movements of the eyes are influenced almost totally by extralinguistic factors, that is, fixations are made at regular intervals determined by the oculomotor system and not on the basis of information extracted from the features of the text. If this model of eye movement behavior were tenable, then dramatic increases in reading rates could be achieved by training readers to move their eyes greater distances before making a fixation.

Low-level control models suggest that the eye is guided to certain locations in the text on the basis of gross visual characteristics. This model has been supported by evidence collected in experiments dealing with the visual search of pictures (see, for example, Mackworth and Morandi 1967).

In the oculomotor scanning of pictures, the eye is directed largely to the areas that hold the most visual information, whereas in reading the eye would be guided to longer words. The picture search task, however, is not likely to generate an adequate model for reading eye movements as it is abundantly clear that the important features of a picture are more easily isolated than the important linguistic features of text.

High-level control models, such as hypothesis-testing theories of reading, hold that the eye is guided by higher level processing mechanisms that analyze the syntactic and semantic features of the text. The reader makes hypotheses based on his acquired knowledge of the orthographic, phonetic, syntactic, and semantic combinations possible in the reader's language. The knowledge of these redundancies allows the reader to skip regions of text and fixate an area not likely to be redundant and therefore carries a considerable amount of information.

Process-monitoring control models view the eye guidance system as being controlled by a buffer that holds and analyzes visual information and triggers an eye movement when further visual information is ready for processing. A related process-monitoring model that does not require the existence of a visual buffer is the unbuffered processing model. According to this model, the processing of visual and contextual information includes the area of fixation and includes all information to the right of fixation that can be analyzed at some criterion level of certainty. When processing of this region is finished, the eye is guided to a point outside the region in which identification has been achieved.

Mixed models include aspects of previously described models such as a model that suggests the direct perception of information during the fixation and the guiding of eye movement by the peripheral text pattern.

Rayner and McConkie (1976, for example) have conducted series of studies intended to describe the fixation patterns and the peripheral cues that determine the perceptual span. Their results show that peripheral cues such as word length, word shape, and visual features influence the placement of the next saccadic eye movement. The reader obtains lexical or semantic information for words in foveal vision. Visual featural information can be discriminated from parafoveal vision whereas gross visual characteristics (such as word length and word outline) are available out as far as five degrees from fixation. These results suggest a model of eye guidance involving an integrative visual buffer that stores information used by the reader for the nonrandom control of eye movements.

Clinical studies of disturbed oculomotor function have indicated that the brain mechanisms that subserve the reading process have a great potential for functional adaptation. Several cases of congenital ophthalmoplegia (Moebius syndrome) have been reported in the clinical literature and reveal that, despite mild reactions in intelligence and the inability to make lateral or medial eye movements, some of these children are able to function at age level in reading (see, for example, Kalverboer et al. 1970; Stebbins et al. 1975). Further, there is evidence to suggest that normal reading comprehension can be achieved in cases of nystagmus and neurological disorders affecting oculomotor control (Ciuffreda et al. 1976). These observations demonstrate that saccadic eye movements are not necessary for fluent reading even though they play such an important role in the normal reading model. Functional adaptations in reading strategies can compensate for oculomotor dysfunction.

Recently, the role of eye movements in reading disability has been a topic of great concern to educators, psychologists, and neuroscientists. Although disturbed reading eye movements have been suggested as a possible etiology of congenital forms of reading disability (see, for example, Zangwill and Blakemore 1972), attempts to train children to make regular eye movements have not been conspicuously successful in remediating reading difficulty. These results will be discussed extensively in conjunction with the results of the reading eye movement recordings of subjects in the present volume.

Previous research with disabled readers (Tinker 1958; Mosse and Daniels 1959; Rubino and Minden 1973) revealed that their eye movements during reading differ significantly from normals in the following respects:

Disabled readers make an increased number of fixations per line of text.

Disabled readers have an increased number of regressions.

Disabled readers have longer fixation durations.

Disabled readers show return sweep inaccuracies.

Disabled readers have periods of confusion with many short regressions and foward movements intermixed.

Recent case studies (Pirozzolo and Rayner 1978b; Pirozzolo et al. 1977a; Pirozzolo and Rayner 1978a) that have treated developmental dyslexia not as a single homogeneous entity but as at least two independent neurobehavioral syndromes have found an interesting relationship between reading eye movements and dyslexia.  These studies indicated that auditory-linguistic dyslexics show a pattern of eye movement typical of young children just learning to read, that is, increased number of fixations, fixation durations, and regressions. When these dyslexics read easy text they showed a normal eye movement pattern. It cannot be contended on the basis of these observations that dyslexia in these children is caused by abnormal eye movements (it may be argued instead that the apparent abnormal eye movements in these children are caused by dyslexia).

The apparently delayed oculomotor pattern manifested by these dyslexics illustrates a difficulty in making rapid grapheme-to-phoneme and lexical associations.

These case studies have also indicated that visual-spatial dyslexics do show a very atypical reading eye movement pattern. The most outstanding feature that can be observed from an eye movement record is the tendency to scan a line of text in a leftward direction. The reverse staircase movement is probably associated with a spatial disorder; it is as yet unclear as to whether this form of dyslexia can be attributed to an eye movement disorder. Due to evidence of other spatial problems (such as directional disorientation) in these patients, it appears that the spatial mechanism that guides the eye--rather than the oculomotor mechanism itself--is the causal factor. Increased numbers of regressions, right-to-left scanning patterns, and instances of return sweep inaccuracies indicate that the mechanisms that serve the functions of visual orientation and integration are sending inaccurate information about the targets for subsequent saccades.

PROPOSED RESEARCH

The research to be described in the following sections deals with the relationship of dyslexia to certain selected visual information-processing variables. One of the assumptions in this research is that there are at least two subgroups of developmental dyslexia, an auditory-linguistic dyslexia and a visual-spatial dyslexia. It is hoped that, by illustrating the various deficits in each of these forms of reading disability, evidence will accrue toward the support of the position that the two dyslexias are indeed independent neuropsychological syndromes. Further, it is assumed that this research may have implications for the normal reading process because the study of normal skilled reading will be enhanced by the investigation of the patterns of impairment to which these skills are subject.

The major purpose of the first task was to investigate the following two assumption: (1) that auditory-linguistic dyslexics do not show the normal right visual field superiority in a visual hemifield task and that the patterns of performance may distinguish between the two groups of dyslexics as well as suggest a possible deficiency that is different for each group; (2) that visual-spatial dyslexics have a smaller span from which useful visual information can be acquired, whereas auditory-linguistic dyslexics have a general word recognition defect for information that occurs in parafoveal vision to the right of fixation.

The major purpose of the second task was to investigate the assumption that there is a connection between oculomotor reaction time and the visual-spatial form of reading impairment. Normal readers show a significantly shorter latency for eye movements to the right. Greater saccadic latencies for initiating right-going movements by dyslexics may indicate that the reading process is being disrupted by increasing the amount of time necessary to make normal left-to-right reading eye movements.

The final task was designed to test the assumption that eye movements are a source of difficulty for dyslexics. Literature review reveals that dyslexics differ from normals in the following aspects of oculomotor behavior during reading:

Fixation durations are longer.
There are more instances of return sweep inaccuracies.
There are more instances of regressions and faulty right-to-left scanning.
There are an increased number of fixations per line of text.

Pirozzolo et al. (1977a) showed that auditory-linguistic dyslexics do not differ from normals in their eye movement behavior during the reading of easy text. It is suggested, however, that the eye movement behavior of visual-spatial dyslexics is different in that there are increased numbers of faulty right-to-left scanning and return sweep inaccuracies in the eye movement records of these children. The visual disorientation that accompanies these eye movement phenomena is believed to hinder the reading process by making it difficult to maintain the necessary order, continuity, and integration of visual images necessary for fluent reading.

3 RESEARCH

SUBJECTS

Twenty-four male subjects with a mean age of 11.1 years served as subjects in each of the tasks in this study. Because handedness has been demonstrated to be an important factor (and may be an important source of variance in other studies) in tasks similar to the ones designed for this study (Rayner and Pirozzolo 1978; Selnes 1977; Hardyck and Petrinovich 1977), only right-handed subjects were employed. Handedness was assessed by the Edinburgh Inventory (Oldfield 1971). Two clinical groups of dyslexics were matched with control subjects for age and full-scale IQ. All subjects had normal vision and hearing as assessed by recent school screenings. Dyslexics had reading diagnostic test scores at least two years below their chronological age norms, whereas normal readers were at grade level or slightly above. Reading test scores were obtained from school officials and were compared for compatibility to results obtained in a brief screening test performed several days before the beginning of these experiments. The tests used include the Wide Range Achievement Test (Jastak and Jastak 1965), the Gray Oral Reading Test (Gray 1963), and the Spache Diagnostic Reading Scales (Spache 1963). In addition, dyslexics were selected from large clinical and school populations and assigned to one of the following two clinical groups based on behavioral descriptions, writing samples (see Figures 3.1 and 3.2), and psychological and neuropsychological test results (see Table 3.1).

Auditory-linguistic dyslexics were subjects whose predominant difficulty in reading was in understanding the phonological characteristics of the visual features of text. These children made

FIGURE 3.1

Handwriting Sample

NAME Ci hicr

What is the first month of the year? January

What is the last month of the year? December

What month do we start school? September

What month is your birthday? JANUary 10

What month is Halloween in? OCTober

What holiday is in May? mothers

What is the last holiday of the year? Christmas

What is the last month of the school? Juh

How many months are in one year? 12

What is the first holiday of the year? new Keer DAY

Put the holidays in the right order:

P	Thanksgiving	2	Valentine's Day
1	New Year's Day	6	Father's Day
3	St. Patrick's Day	10	Christmas
8	Halloween	4	Easter
7	4th of July	5	Mother's Day

Source: Compiled by the author.

FIGURE 3.2

Geometric Drawing Sample

Source: Compiled by the author.

TABLE 3.1

Mean Age, IQ, and Reading Level for Subjects

	Normal Readers	Auditory-Linguistic Dyslexics	Visual-Spatial Dyslexics
Age	11.0	11.1	11.2
Full-scale IQ	106	103	105
Verbal IQ	106	96	113
Performance IQ	107	113	94
Reading level	5.8	2.9	3.1

Source: Compiled by the author.

considerably more grapheme-to-phoneme translation errors during oral reading (and phoneme-to-grapheme correspondence errors in spelling) than other errors. They had a lower mean verbal IQ than controls or visual-spatial dyslexics and other symptoms of language disorders such as late onset of speech, anomia, speech discrimination problems, and agrammatism.

Visual-spatial dyslexics were subjects whose deficits in reading were characterized by a difficulty in discriminating and analyzing the visual features of text. Despite the fact that the mean age for this group was 11.2 years, letter and word reversals continued to be a source of difficulty. Paralexias that involved letter confusions, omissions, and reversals predominated in the records of the visual-spatial group. These children had a lower mean performance IQ than controls or auditory-linguistic dyslexics and other symptoms of disordered visual-spatial functioning such as right-left disorientation, spatial dysgraphia, and dyscalculia.

APPARATUS

The first two tasks described in this chapter employed a NOVA 12/20 digital computer with 16,000 words of memory, 2 discs, an A-D and D-A converter, and a CRT. A Biometrics Model 200-1 eye movement monitor was interfaced with the computer so that a sampling of eye position was taken 1,000 times per second. The eye  movement monitor is a photoelectric device that registers the amount of reflected light between the iris and the sclera of the eye. Two sets of three transducers that are mounted on spectacle frames are placed close to the subject's eye. One set is fixed so that the photocells are aimed at the center of the pupil and at the two horizontal iris-sclera boundaries. Thus, when the eye moves horizontally one photocell will receive less reflected light than the opposing photocell, which would then be detecting the white sclera. These measurements result in a net current that is a function of the eye's deflection to the right or left. Output from the photosensors is then converted to digital values by an A-D converter and processed by the computer.

Horizontal eye movements were recorded from the left eye. Vertical eye movement detection was not done because stimuli were presented on a horizontal plane. The system is capable of vertical eye movement monitoring, although it is much less accurate than the horizontal measurements.

Pilot work with this system indicated that reliable measurements of eye movement latencies could be made if threshold eye movement amplitude were set at 30 minutes of visual angle. Thus, the computer ignored any small movements of the eyes, such as tremors and drifts, and recorded an eye movement when eye position had changed by 30 minutes.

Task 3 used both the Biometrics eye movement monitor and a strip chart recorder to detect and record reading eye movements.

PROCEDURE

When the subjects arrived for the experimental session, they were taken into a soundproof room adjacent to the room that housed the computer. The subjects were seated in front of the CRT, which was interfaced with the computer. A chin rest and forehead rest were used to keep the head relatively still and maintain a distance of 16 inches from the display screen to the eye.

After the subjects were seated, the first task involving foveal and parafoveal word recognition was explained to them. The experimenter controlled the display with a button and when the subject was ready, a fixation cross appeared in the middle of the CRT for 500 milliseconds followed by a three-letter stimulus word that appeared for 125 milliseconds. The words were presented in one of five locations on the CRT: in the central fovea so that the middle letter of the three-letter word appeared in the same character position as the fixation cross (thus, the word began at -0.5 and ended at +0.5), beginning at one degree to the right of fixation, beginning at two degrees to the right of fixation, ending one degree to the left of fixation, and ending two degrees to the left of fixation. Sixteen words were used in the task and each appeared once at each of the five locations on the CRT. There were 80 trials. The presentation order of the location of the words was randomly varied among the five points by the computer.

Each subject was told that words would appear to the right and left of a central fixation point and that he should attempt to keep his eyes fixated on the cross because his performance could not be improved by guessing from which direction the word would appear. Subject responses were recorded immediately after the disappearance of the stimulus.

The three-letter stimulus words used in this task were reversible (for example, was, now, are, but). It was thought that these stimuli might lend themselves to the analysis of the problem of reversals. In particular, one way of assessing the relationship between abnormal right-to-left scanning during reading and reversals would be to compare performance in the right visual field, which demands left-to-right scanning, with performance in the left visual field, which demands right-to-left scanning. Although the results of this attempt were suggestive (75 percent of the word reversals made were in the left visual field), too few reversals (2 percent) were made at the relatively long exposure duration of 125 milliseconds and thus no further conclusions were drawn.

After the completion of task 1, each subject was given a five-minute break. Following the rest period, calibration of the eye movement sensors was done. The spectacle frames were placed on the subject and he was realigned in the chin rest so that the glabella was 16 inches from the CRT. The sensors were fixed by means of a calibration pattern that detected the deflection of the eye as it moved equal distances to the right and left of the central fixation cross.

Calibration typically lasted from three to five minutes and was followed by an explanation of the task demands to the subject. The two conditions of this task were counterbalanced so that the odd-numbered subjects of each group completed a word condition first and a symbol condition second, and the even-numbered subjects completed the symbol condition first and the word condition second. In the word condition, as in the previous task, the experimenter presented a fixation cross to start the trial. In this task, however, a subsequent button press by the experimenter was needed to trigger the stimulus. This enabled the experimenter to note when the subject's eyes had returned to the fixation cross position (as indicated by the deflection of the Biometrics eye movement monitor, which had previously been carefully calibrated). The trial began when the subject fixated the cross. In the word condition, one of the three-letter words used in the first task appeared in one of eight locations on the CRT: beginning two, three, five, or ten degrees to the right of fixation or ending two, three, five, or ten degrees to the left of fixation. The visual angle at which the words appeared was randomly varied by the computer. In the symbol condition, the fixation cross was followed by the number symbol (#) at one of the eight locations. Visual angle was again random among the eight points. Each of the stimuli was presented for three seconds. When the stimulus disappeared the examiner pressed a button to start the cycle again. The subjects were instructed to move their eyes to the stimulus and, in the word condition, to name the word. There were 64 trials in each condition. The subject was given a short break between conditions that lasted about three minutes. Recalibration was accomplished following the break and the second condition of this task was run.

Analog-to-digital conversion of data was made at the rate of 1,000 sampling points per second by the NOVA 12/20 digital computer. The millisecond clock was started simultaneously with the exposure of the stimulus and stopped when the subject made a saccade of 30 minutes or more. Pilot research, as well as evidence collected in other saccadic latency studies (for example, Baloh and Honrubia 1976), indicated that trials in which the reaction time exceeded 400 milliseconds were representative of an error involving the amplitude threshold for an eye movement or an error involving fixation control. Trials that resulted in reaction times exceeding 400 milliseconds were very infrequent (2 percent of the total number of data points) and were deleted from the data. Similarly, trials that resulted in reaction times of less than 100 milliseconds were scored as "guesses," representing anticipatory saccades, and were also deleted from the data (guesses totaled 5 percent of the total number of data points). It is perhaps clinically interesting that visual-spatial dyslexics experienced greater difficulty in maintaining fixation prior to stimulus onset than either of the other groups. This observation supports the results of a study by Cohen and Ross (1977), who found that poor readers were less able than good readers to maintain fixation on a target.

After completion of the second condition of the saccadic latency task the subjects were given another short rest period. Recalibration of the photosensors was done and an explanation of the final task was given. Subjects were told that they would read two paragraphs of text and that their eye movements would be recorded and printed out by the strip chart recorder. As each read from passages in the Gray Oral Reading Test (Gray 1963), form B, horizontal saccadic eye movements of the left eye were measured by a Biometrics Model 200-1 eye movement monitor and a strip chart recorder. All subjects read two passages--one considerably below their measured reading level and the other between one and two years above their reading level. Reading material was chosen on the basis of the reading level determined by testing. The experimenter noted in the eye movement record places where the subject made errors in decoding, pronunciation, omissions, or substitutions. The page of text subtended approximately 12.5 degrees of visual angle when held at a comfortable viewing distance.

After the experimental session the strip chart recordings of the subjects' reading eye movements were scored with respect to the four dependent variables previously discussed: fixation duration, fixation frequency, regression frequency, and return sweep inaccuracies. Fixation durations were computed by dividing the number of fixations into the total time spent in fixation (the amount of time that the eye was in flight was subtracted out of the record using mean values from Rayner 1978a). This procedure differs from others, such as those of Rubino and Minden (1973), who fail to account for the length of time the eye is in motion and therefore these results are thought to be a more accurate estimate of the actual mean fixation durations. Return sweep inaccuracies were defined as dysmetric saccades that were inaccurate by at least two degrees on the return sweep or return sweeps that were accomplished by a series of right-to-left saccades.

RESULTS

Foveal and Parafoveal Word Identification

Table 3.2 illustrates the mean percentage of correct word identifications at each of the five locations in the first task. A 3 (reading group) x 5 (visual location) analysis of variance was carried out on the percentage of correct responses. The analysis yielded significant main effects of reading group, $F(2,21) = 5.92$, $p < .01$, and visual location, $F(4,84) = 26.01$, $p < .001$. A Newman Keuls Test indicated that the mean percentage of correct identifications for the normal readers (90.8) and the auditory-linguistic dyslexics (88.5) was significantly greater than the mean percentage of correct identifications for the visual-spatial dyslexics (83.9). A Newman Keuls Test on the main effect of visual location indicated that performance for words presented two degrees to the left of fixation (79 percent) did not differ from performance at two degrees to the right (82 percent) although these values were significantly different ($p < .05$) from performance at one degree to the left of fixation (89 percent) and one degree to the right (91 percent), which did not differ from each other. Foveal performance differed from that at one degree ($p < .05$) and at two degrees ($p < .05$), but the percentage correct in foveal vision was nearly perfect for each group (mean 97 percent).

TABLE 3.2

Mean Percentage of Correct Word Identifications

	Left, Degrees			Right, Degrees	
	2	1	Fovea	1	2
Normal readers	82	90	97	96	88
Auditory-linguistic dyslexics	83	91	97	89	81
Visual-spatial dyslexics	73	85	96	89	72

Source: Compiled by the author.

In order to understand the pattern of effects more precisely, a further 3 (reading group) x 2 (visual field) x 2 (visual angle) analysis of variance was carried out in which the percentage of correct identifications for foveally presented words was not included. This was done in order to determine the nature of any interactions between visual field, visual angle, and reading group. What is of most interest in this analysis is the effects of the within-subject variables: visual field and visual angle. There were significant main effects of each of these variables, $F(1,21) = 4.72$, $p < .05$ and 27.89, $p < .001$ for visual field and visual angle, respectively. Figure 3.3 illustrates the mean percentage of correct word identifications at each of four locations. Subjects were more accurate in identifying words presented to the right visual field (87 percent) than those presented to the left (84 percent) and words presented one degree from fixation were more accurately identified (90 percent) than words presented two degrees (81 percent). Finally, there was a marginally significant interaction of reading group x visual field, $F(2,21) = 3.32$, $p < .055$. This interaction, which can be seen in Figure 3.4, resulted from similar performance patterns by the normal and visual-spatial dyslexics (with the latter group considerably poorer than the former) coupled with a different pattern by the auditory-linguistic group. Generally, the normals and visual-spatial groups were more accurate for words presented to the right visual field whereas the auditory-linguistic group showed a symmetrical pattern and performance in both visual fields was comparable.

Saccadic Eye Movement Reaction Times

Tables 3.3 and 3.4 show the saccadic latency means at the eight locations for each of the three groups in each of the two conditions. The data are derived from approximately 120 data points for each of the eight subjects in each group. A 3 (reading group) x 2 (task: words vs. symbols) x 2 (saccade direction) x 4 (visual angle) analysis of variance was carried out on the mean saccadic reaction times. This analysis yielded significant main effects of task, $F(1,21) = 16.05$, $p < .001$, saccade direction, $F(1,21) = 8.24$, $p < .01$, and visual angle, $F(3,63) = 5.70$, $p < .01$. A Newman Keuls Test on the main effect of visual angle indicated that mean reaction time to stimuli appearing at two degrees (213 milliseconds) and 10 degrees (210 milliseconds) did not differ from each other but did differ significantly from the means at three degrees (200 milliseconds) and five degrees (201 milliseconds), $p < .05$. Saccades to the right were faster (202 milliseconds) than saccades to the left (210 milliseconds) and words resulted in shorter latencies (199 milliseconds) than the symbols (213 milliseconds).

FIGURE 3.3

Visual Half-field Test Results

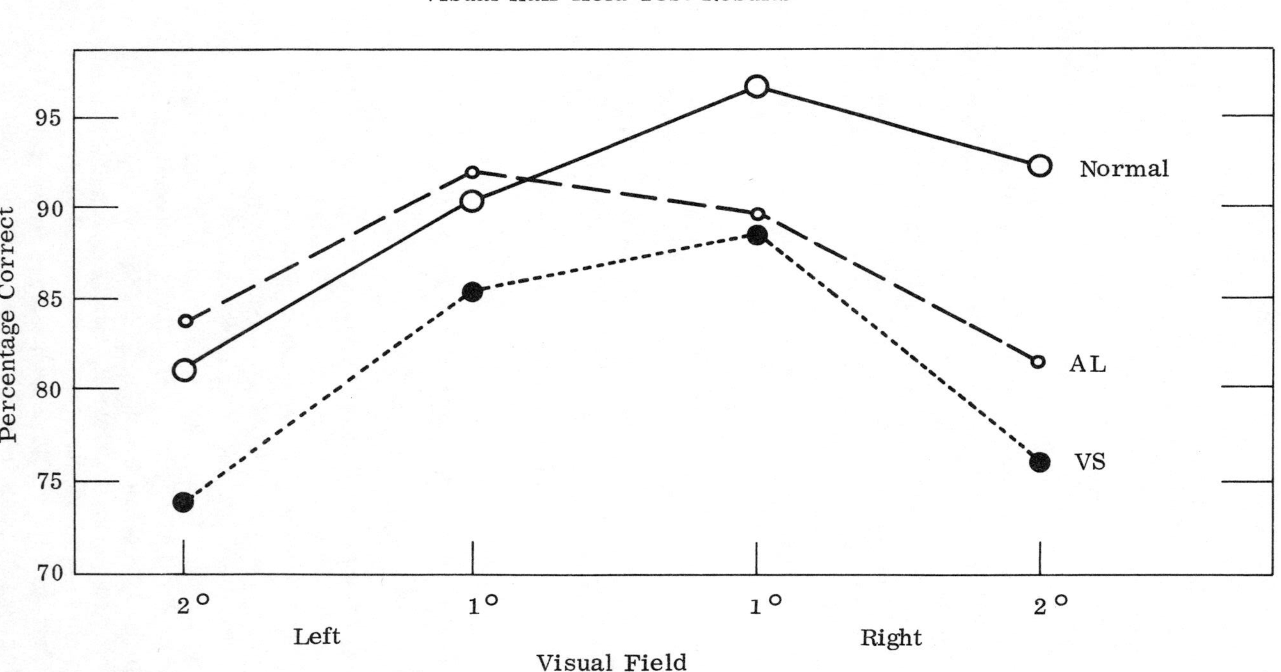

Source: Constructed by the author.

FIGURE 3.4

Saccadic Eye Movement Reaction Time Test Results

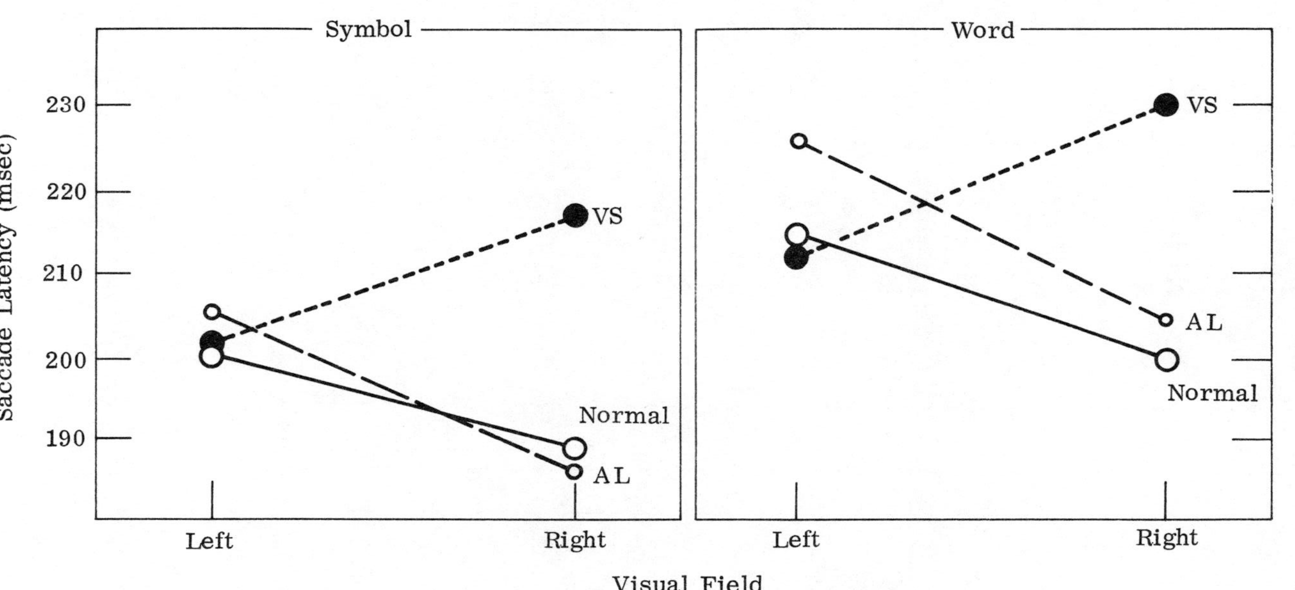

Source: Constructed by the author.

TABLE 3.3

Saccadic Reaction Time for Word Condition
(milliseconds)

	Left				Right				
	2	3	5	10	2	3	5	10	$\overline{X}$
Normal readers	198	199	196	210	195	178	187	187	194
Auditory-linguistic dyslexics	198	205	203	222	199	190	175	176	196
Visual-spatial dyslexics	201	186	197	215	206	217	207	233	208
	199	197	198	216	200	194	190	199	200

Source: Compiled by the author.

TABLE 3.4

Saccadic Reaction Time for Symbol Condition
(milliseconds)

	Left				Right				
	2	3	5	10	2	3	5	10	$\overline{X}$
Normal readers	198	205	211	222	210	207	184	198	204
Auditory-linguistic dyslexics	236	224	212	240	218	203	190	205	216
Visual-spatial dyslexics	217	198	219	209	232	214	220	242	219
	223	207	214	224	220	208	198	212	213

Source: Compiled by the author.

TABLE 3.5

Eye Movements and Fixations during Reading

	Normal readers	Auditory-linguistic dyslexics	Visual-spatial dyslexics
Mean number of fixations per line			
Easy	6.0	5.7	6.3
Difficult	7.8	7.8	7.6
Average fixation duration			
Easy	252	274	273
Difficult	260	273	274
Mean number of return sweep inaccuracies			
Easy	.50	.75	2.6
Difficult	.62	.75	2.75
Mean percentage of regressions			
Easy	15.1	22.2	22.2
Difficult	21.8	27.7	24.7

Source: Compiled by the author.

Although there was no significant main effect of reading group ($F < 1$), there was a highly significant interaction of reading group x saccade direction, ($F(2,21) = 22.89$, $p < .0001$. This interaction can be seen in Figure 3.4 and was due to the fact that normal readers and auditory-linguistic dyslexics had shorter reaction times to stimuli in the right visual field whereas the visual-spatial group had shorter reaction times to the left. This is the most salient result to be derived from the data. Normal readers had a mean saccadic reaction time of 192 milliseconds to stimuli appearing in the right visual field and a mean of 207 milliseconds to left-field stimuli. Similarly, auditory-linguistic dyslexics had a mean reaction time of 194 milliseconds to right visual field stimuli and 217 milliseconds to the left visual field stimuli. Visual-spatial dyslexics showed precisely the opposite pattern, responding to right visual field stimuli in 221 milliseconds and left-field stimuli in 205 milliseconds.

Reading Eye Movements

Table 3.5 shows the results of the scoring of the reading eye movement records for the three groups in the two conditions (easy vs. difficult text). Separate analyses were carried out on three of the dependent variables: fixation duration, number of regressions, and number of return sweep inaccuracies. A 3 (reading group) x 2 (task: easy vs. difficult) analysis of variance revealed that the number of regressions increased with text difficulty, $F(1, 21) = 11.02$, $p < .01$. No significant differences between tasks were found for fixation duration or return sweep inaccuracies. There was, however, a between-subjects main effect of groups for return sweep inaccuracies, $F(2,21) = 0.42$, $p < .001$ and a Newman Keuls Test revealed that the visual-spatial group made significantly more ($p < .01$) return sweep inaccuracies than either the auditory-linguistic dyslexics or normal readers, who did not differ from each other. Between-subjects analysis of variance for number of fixations was not done because of the task characteristics. Text from the Gray Oral Reading Test changes in certain of its visual characteristics (for example, B-2 text type is larger with shorter and fewer words than subsequent passages, which are progressively more difficult) that are known to influence eye movement and fixational characteristics (Rayner and McConkie 1977).

4 DISCUSSION

This chapter will present a discussion of the results presented in the previous chapter and the implications of these results for the neuropsychological analysis of developmental dyslexia. The principal findings of this study were:

Normal readers had nearly perfect word recognition for simple, short words presented in the fovea for brief (125 millisecond) intervals. Recognition was better for these linguistic elements when they were presented in the right visual field rather than in the left and better when words were displaced by one degree than by two degrees.

Auditory-linguistic dyslexics identified simple, short words with near perfect accuracy when they were briefly presented in the fovea. There was no lateral asymmetry in the word recognition process for these dyslexics. Words presented one degree from fixation were recognized more accurately than words presented two degrees from fixation and this effect was demonstrable in both visual fields.

Like the two other groups, visual-spatial dyslexics identified simple, short words briefly presented in foveal vision with near perfect accuracy. Word recognition was better in the right visual field than the left and there was a more pronounced decrement in performance at two degrees (vs. performance at one degree) than for either of the other groups.

Normal readers had shorter eye movement latencies for saccades going from left to right than saccades going from right to left. Reaction time was faster with words that were presented in parafoveal and peripheral vision than with a number symbol that had less visual information than the three-letter words.

Auditory-linguistic dyslexics had shorter eye movement latencies for rightward saccades than for saccades going in a leftward direction and thus showed the same pattern as normal readers.

Visual-spatial dyslexics had shorter eye movement latencies for leftward saccades than for saccades going in a rightward direction. Reaction time was faster with three-letter words than to a number symbol.

Saccadic reaction time was faster with words or symbols that were presented at three or five degrees than to these stimuli presented at two or ten degrees.

Normal readers made more fixations and short regressions when text was difficult than when text was easy. No change was observed in the number of return sweep inaccuracies (very infrequent for this group) and in fixation duration.

Auditory-linguistic dyslexics made more fixations and short regressions when text was difficult than when text was easy. When text difficulty is carefully controlled there are probably no differences in the values for fixation duration, fixation frequency, and regression frequency between normal readers and this group of dyslexics. Return sweep inaccuracies were very infrequent for this group in either the easy text or difficult text condition.

Visual-spatial dyslexics made an increased number of fixations and short regressions when text difficulty was increased. This group made a larger number of return sweep inaccuracies (including instances of right-to-left scanning) but the number of return sweep inaccuracies did not vary with text difficulty.

In summary, across the three tasks discussed in this volume the major differences between the three groups were that auditory-linguistic dyslexics differed from normal readers in that they showed no lateral asymmetry for word recognition and that the visual-spatial dyslexics differed from normals in that they showed a general word recognition defect when words were presented in parafoveal vision, that they had a faster saccadic reaction time for leftward eye movements, and that they showed a large number of return sweep inaccuracies when reading text.

DYSLEXIA AND LATERAL ASYMMETRIES IN VISUAL PERCEPTION

The results of this study replicated those of Marcel et al. (1974), Kershner (1977), Witelson (1977), and Pirozzolo and Rayner (1979). Auditory-linguistic dyslexics did not exhibit the right visual field superiority observed in normal readers. This finding appears to support the assumption that linguistic processing within the left hemisphere is less efficiently carried out in auditory-linguistic dyslexics than in normal readers. Performance in the left visual field by the auditory-linguistic dyslexics did not differ from that of normal readers, thus suggesting an equivalence of right hemisphere linguistic function between the auditory-linguistic dyslexics and normals. This evidence would not support the theory proposed by Marcel et al. that the right hemisphere is the source of the dyslexic deficit because of its superior linguistic ability.

Visual-spatial dyslexics did exhibit a pronounced right visual field superiority, although their performance is considerably poorer than normals at all parafoveal locations in both left and right visual fields. Under slightly different conditions such as shortening the exposure duration to threshold levels for each subject (that is, less than 50 milliseconds for most subjects) the asymmetry exhibited by this group may well increase to the level reported by Yeni-Komshian et al. (1975). Dyslexics in their study had larger right visual field superiorities than normal readers and these authors argued that dyslexia may be caused by a right hemisphere dysfunction or a callosal syndrome that degrades the transmission of information across the commissures. Very little evidence would seem to support the former explanation, although the later explanation has been advanced (Beaumont 1976) and would appear, in part, to fit the data reported in the present study. Although visual hemifield studies can reveal neural events of various stages, neither the present study nor the investigation reported by Yeni-Komshian et al. is conclusive evidence that the information transfer (that is, the commissural) stage is the causal factor in the word recognition deficit manifested by dyslexics, since these studies fail to separate the information reception, processing, transfer, or output stages.

Interestingly, however, two lesions are necessary to produce the reading deficit in the agnosic (or pure) form of acquired dyslexia. Lesions involving the splenium and the left visual association region combine to produce the disconnection syndrome of agnosic alexia (Dejerine 1891; Benson and Geschwind 1969). Not surprisingly, the corpus callosum and the angular gyrus areas are among the last brain regions to reach anatomical maturity (Yakovlev and Lecours 1967; Lecours 1975; Flechsig 1901; Selnes 1974). Certainly, the nature of the pathophysiology is obscure because of the numerous neurophysiological and histochemical factors that govern brain function, but recent evidence (Lecours 1975; Milner 1976) demonstrated some very interesting parallels between neuroanatomical maturation and the appearance of behavioral stages of development.

DYSLEXIA AND SACCADIC EYE MOVEMENT REACTION TIMES

Launay (1952) found that certain dyslexics were able to read a series of letters more rapidly from right to left than from left to right and that this behavior persisted into adulthood. This observation was among the first demonstrations indicating that there may be a subgroup of dyslexics who show basic oculomotor abnormalities. Other evidence has been reviewed that supports this view and questions numerous reports that have concluded that oculomotor factors do not contribute to the variability in reading ability. The researchers adopting the latter position have contended that the simple oculomotor skill necessary for reading is overlearned by the time children learn to read. Similarly, Spache (1976) suggested that beginning readers have a fundamental oculomotor skill that is well developed and there is no developmental trend toward improvement in this ability. Neither suggestion (that there is no developmental trend toward improving oculomotor function and that basic oculomotor ability is unrelated to the syndrome of developmental dyslexia) receives support from the evidence gathered by researchers interested in saccadic eye movement latencies.

Lesevre (1964) established that there are two developmental trends in oculomotor activity that unfold between the ages of six and 12. First, oculomotor reaction time decreases progressively between these ages and there is evidence of a small decrease from age 12 into adulthood. Second, the "right lateralization of gaze" becomes established around age seven and increases slowly until adulthood. The oculomotor functions that are asymmetric and show developmental trends include saccadic reaction time (faster to the right), whereas oculomotor efficiency and eye stability are superior when scanning is in a rightward direction. In her electrooculographic study of dyslexic children with delayed spatial functions (who presumably correspond to the visual-spatial dyslexics in the present study), Lesevre found an absence of right gaze lateralization and, in some cases, a left lateralization (such as decreased reaction time to the left).

Although the present study does not provide direct evidence that there is a progressive shortening of oculomotor reaction time, comparison of the latencies in this study with other studies using adult subjects (Rayner 1978a; Baloh and Honrubia 1976) and a subsequent study (Rayner and Pirozzolo 1978) of adult performance on the tasks reported in the present communication suggests that there is a shortening of latencies from age 11 into adulthood. Latencies in the present study average 206 milliseconds whereas Rayner reports mean latencies of 178 milliseconds, Baloh and Honrubia report latencies of 186 milliseconds, and Rayner and Pirozzolo report latencies of 180 milliseconds. Further, Cohen and Ross (1977) used both children (mean age 8.7) and adults and found that reaction time for adults was approximately 20 milliseconds shorter than that for children.

Consistent with the results of Lesevre's study, the visual-spatial dyslexics in this study exhibited shorter saccadic latencies for right-to-left eye movements. The mean reaction times for this group to stimuli presented at two, three, five, and ten degrees was approximately 213 milliseconds and were therefore inconsistent with the results of the study by Dossetor and Papaioannou (1975), who found reaction times of 500 milliseconds for their undifferentiated group of dyslexics. Even though saccades were made to points 40 degrees from fixation in the Dossetor and Papaioannou study, it is unclear as to why reaction time is so long since latencies should be only slightly longer than those for amplitudes of ten degrees (Baloh and Honrubia 1976).

Visual-spatial dyslexics showed shorter latencies to left visual field stimuli, suggesting that processing within the right hemisphere was more efficient than processing within the left hemisphere. These results imply that visuomotor processing in the left hemisphere is abnormally slow, and thus the theory that a dysfunction involving the left visual association areas was supported (this task did not involve interhemispheric transfer, and therefore no implications can be drawn about callosal functions). Auditory-linguistic dyslexics showed a pattern similar to normal readers and thus no involvement of the visuomotor pathways is speculated.

Good readers exhibited faster reaction times for making left-to-right saccades but the reasons for this asymmetry have not been established. Rayner (1978a) pointed out that one reason for shorter latencies for rightward saccades may simply be that readers make 90 percent of saccades during reading from left to right. Although this is one plausible explanation, it is unlikely that reading habits are the only contributing factor in this asymmetry. An alternative explanation implicates the role of handedness in the asymmetry and some recent evidence upholds this hypothesis.

Rayner and Pirozzolo (1978) demonstrated that left-handers show no asymmetry for saccadic latencies. This observation suggests that the superior visuomotor organization of the right-handers' left cerebral hemisphere (which initiates rightward saccades) reduces the amount of time necessary to program and launch a rightward saccade, as compared to the amount of time it takes the right hemisphere to program and launch a leftward saccade. As a group, left-handers do not show a lateral asymmetry, a result that is predictable on the basis of what is hypothesized about left-handers and the conspicuously absent single pattern of performance in perceptual and cognitive tasks (Hardyck and Petrinovich 1977).

Saccadic eye movement reaction times to stimuli at three and five degrees were shorter than reaction times to stimuli at two and ten degrees. Similarly, Rayner (1978a) found that reaction times decrease from one to five degrees. It appears that stimuli, such as words, in parafoveal vision are subject to an increased amount of neural processing (as opposed to stimuli in the periphery) because a greater amount of visual information is available. Reaction time to words that are at three or five degrees may be faster because there is little useful visual information that can be abstracted by the cortical receptive mechanisms. Another possibility is that the superior colliculus, which is more adept than the mechanisms of the geniculocalcarine system at locating objects in the periphery (Wurtz and Mohler 1974), is selecting the peripheral targets and triggering eye movements. The participation of the cerebral cognitive mechanisms in the eye movements made during this task may be a linearly decreasing function of the amount of useful visual information. The transition to the more efficient visually guided eye movement system driven by the superior colliculus at more eccentric points in parafoveal and peripheral vision would decrease reaction time until a point further in the periphery (between five and ten degrees) where reaction time increases as a function of fewer receptive cells acting on the visual system.

DYSLEXIA AND READING EYE MOVEMENTS

The results of the present study demonstrated a close relationship between measures of eye movements (such as fixation and regression frequency) and text difficulty. Although numerous investigators (such as Rubino and Minden 1973; Taylor 1965) have found that good readers make fewer fixations and regressions than poor readers, the results reported here support the argument that these eye movement characteristics are important to text comprehension. When skilled readers are presented with difficult passages, the measures of eye movements reveal a pattern of increased fixations and regressions. The increased number of fixations and regressions permit the reader to fixate words prior to and following the difficult word in order to examine semantic clues, and thus these eye movement characteristics reflect text difficulty (Bayle 1942; Conant 1964).

When the difficulty of text is carefully controlled, auditory-linguistic dyslexics have eye movement patterns that are very similar to normal readers. Visual-spatial dyslexics, on the other hand, do not show a strong rightward directional attack or accuracy in returning to the first word of the next line after completing the line above. Instances of faulty right-to-left scanning and return sweep inaccuracies are common in the records of these dyslexic children with visual-spatial information-processing disorders. Although it has been suggested that these faulty eye movements cause dyslexia and that remediation of this problem would increase reading ability (Zangwill and Blakemore 1972; Mosse and Daniels 1959), there is no evidence to support this claim. It is more likely that the disordered eye movements are caused by a faulty visual-spatial information-processing system that is also the apparent cause of the reading disability. Other neuropsychological symptoms that sometimes occur in this form of dyslexia, such as directional disorientation, spatial dyscalculia, finger agnosia, spatial dysgraphia, topographical disorientation, and the possibility of a narrower useful field of vision, would clearly suggest this relationship.

The finding that the frequency of return sweep inaccuracies did not change as a function of text difficulty implies that the return sweep, unlike other eye movements during reading, is not under the control of cognitive processes. It appears that it is entirely under the control of the oculomotor system and the spatial mechanism that guides the eye. Visual-spatial dyslexics did not perform the return sweep with the same accuracy as normal readers (or auditory-linguistic dyslexics). It is normal for an individual to undershoot a target in the periphery by a short distance, which then requires a small corrective saccade. This accuracy phenomenon is observable in the reading eye movement records of normals and has been the subject of a recent study of nonreading eye movements by Baloh et al. (1976). They found that saccadic accuracy was in the range of 90 percent and that undershoots and overshoots of 16 percent (the criterion level in the present study) were very rare. Gross undershooting and overshooting is therefore a clinical sign of disturbance involving either the oculomotor system (including the cerebral cortex, basal ganglia, cerebellum, and brain stem) or the cortical visual-spatial system.

A NEUROPSYCHOLOGICAL ANALYSIS OF THE DYSLEXIAS

It has been the purpose of this volume to demonstrate that visual-spatial and oculomotor factors are related to at least one kind of developmental dyslexia. It has been shown that, for a certain small group of dyslexics, disturbances in specific visual information-processing abilities are associated with reading disability. It was concluded that children with a visual-spatial form of dyslexia perform differently on measures of visual-spatial information-processing abilities because of a maturation lag in the neural substrates that govern these functions.

Not considered here were a variety of linguistic defects that may characterize the neuropsychological functioning of the auditory-linguistic group of dyslexics. Previous research (for example, Pirozzolo et al. 1977a; Mattis et al. 1975) suggests that these children may differ from normal readers in the ability to carry out rapid, complex linguistic functions. It is suggested that defects in performance of such tasks as speech shadowing at very short latencies and measures of auditory-linguistic reaction time (such as a lexical decision task) may differentiate this group from normals.

The two forms of developmental dyslexia considered in this volume are probably not the only types of dyslexia to occur in children. Research on acquired cognitive disabilities, such as the aphasias and agnosias, has indicated that disorders at one time considered as a unitary syndrome were eventually shown to be divisible into separate neurobehavioral syndromes. The aphasias, for instance, are divided into separate syndromes, including motor aphasia (also Broca's or expressive), sensory aphasia (also Wernicke's or receptive), conduction aphasia, anomic aphasia, and transcortical motor aphasia.

Other researchers have identified syndromes of dyslexia that do not correspond to those discussed in this volume. As previously mentioned, Boder (1971) identified a third (mixed) form of dyslexia and Mattis et al. (1975) proposed a third (articulation and graphomotor) form. Other attempts to describe neuropsychological syndromes of dyslexia have been made by Frank and Levinson (1976) and Pontius (1976).

There is general agreement among neuropsychologists that the two forms of dyslexia represented in the present study exist as separate clinical entities. These groups bear a modest resemblance to certain acquired neurobehavioral syndromes (Pirozzolo 1977a). The deficits in auditory-linguistic dyslexia are suggestive of a conduction aphasia. Conduction aphasics cannot channel auditory stimuli well enough to direct the frontal mechanisms for speech and writing output. Kinsbourne (1972) found that overloading the conduction aphasic with complex linguistic tasks results in poor performance. This is probably not unlike the disorder in auditory-linguistic dyslexia. Pirozzolo et al. (1977a) showed that the auditory-linguistic dyslexic has a diminished verbal output and a decrement in manual performance when finger tapping is accompanied by simultaneous verbalizing. The psychological deficit in auditory-linguistic dyslexia, as well as in conduction aphasia, appears to be a decrease in efficiency.

The analogy can be extended to account for the mismatching of phonemes and graphemes. Wernicke (1874), who was the first neurologist to recognize the syndrome now known as conduction aphasia (Leitungsaphasie), suggested that the deficits in conduction aphasia were due to the disruption of auditory images. Clinically, it would appear that auditory-linguistic dyslexics are constrained by their inability to reauditorize (Boder 1973) or remember phonemic features of words. It is suggested that the pathway that subserves the transmission of auditory-verbal information is not fully established or space-committed in auditory-linguistic dyslexia.

Visual-spatial dyslexia has previously been described as a congenital form of Gerstmann's syndrome (Hermann and Norrie 1959). In addition to the case for a regional maturation lag in the visual association area, evidence has been presented that may suggest an additional dysfunction somewhat similar to that in the pure form of acquired dyslexia. These neuropsychological correlates and speculations await the results of histological data that may show neuroanatomical or neurophysiological immaturity as the causative factors in developmental dyslexia.

5 NEUROPSYCHOLOGICAL ASSESSMENT

Experienced clinicians stress the importance of very careful psychological examination of children, especially those with learning problems who have a history of inconsistent test performance. Differential diagnosis of developmental disorders by a neuropsychologist, neurologist, or clinical psychologist should include measures of intelligence, memory, language, motor integration, and perception. Previous screening will have separated out those children with brain injuries, sensory defects, personality disorders, and subnormal intelligence. For the child with suspected learning disabilities, general medical examinations by a physician will have provided data on sensory and motor functions, reflexes, and the results of any special tests that were indicated (EEGs, X rays, etc.).

Examiners must be thorough in their testing and cautious about drawing conclusions on the basis of minimal test results. Research has clearly shown that children can suffer not only from the fairly common syndromes of developmental dyslexia, but other developmental disorders of higher cortical function that mimic those occurring in adults with known brain lesions. The excellent work of Tallal (1978) showed that children with developmental aphasia have a variety of defects of an auditory perceptual nature. Clues as to the mechanisms of developmental auditory agnosia, a defect in the ability to recognize nonverbal sounds, have been found recently by Heffner (1977) and by Rapin and her colleagues (1977). In adults it is generally agreed that many more cases of auditory agnosia exist than are recognized but that these agnosias are often mistaken for hearing loss. The literature on learning disabilities is replete with examples of learning-disabled children who have been misclassified as sensory-defective, brain-damaged, and so on. As has been suggested in Chapter 4, many additional forms of developmental disorders of higher cortical function will probably be identified, and a precise understanding of these syndromes will help the clinician to recognize neuropsychological symptomatology in children with learning problems.

A basic screening battery should be designed by the clinician to include tests of each of the aforementioned neuropsychological functions: intelligence, memory, language, motor integration, and perception. Additional special tests should be administered during the course of the examination or in a subsequent session if performance is unsatisfactory, erratic, or otherwise deficient.

TESTS OF INTELLIGENCE

The Wechsler tests of intelligence are the most frequently used psychological tests and are very useful in the assessment of developmental disorders because they include subtests that tap a number of different intellectual functions and because the test can usually be completed in one session of approximately 1-1 1/2 hours. The Wechsler Intelligence Scale for Children-Revised Edition (WISC-R) is a downward extension of the Wechsler Adult Intelligence Scale, providing norms for children between six and 17 years of age. The WISC-R is comprised of two scales of subtests, verbal and performance, with a total of 11 subtests in all. The significance of discrepancies between the verbal scale IQ and performance scale IQ has been a topic of great concern over the years. In general, language abilities are tapped by the verbal subtests and visual perceptual-motor abilities are tapped by the performance subtests. An early discovery in clinical neuropsychology was that left-hemisphere-damaged, language-impaired patients scored relatively more poorly on the verbal portion of the test than on the performance portion, whereas right-hemisphere-damaged, visual-spatial-impaired patients did proportionally worse on the performance scale (Reitan 1955). Rourke and his colleagues (Rourke 1976; Rourke and Telegdy 1975; Rourke, Dietrich and Young 1973) argued that there is some significance also to the finding of verbal-performance discrepancies of more than 15 points in children with learning disabilities. Although this is probably true for the different groups of developmental dyslexia (and there is most certainly a trend in this direction for the research presented in this book), premature conclusions about the qualifications of any one subject for admission to one of the groups of developmental dyslexia should never be reached only on the basis of this observation.

The verbal portion of the WISC-R includes the following subtests: information, vocabulary, comprehension, similarities, arithmetic, and digit span. The information and vocabulary subtests are measures of a general intelligence factor and reflect a child's sociocultural background. The comprehension subtest is a measure of a child's social reasoning ability and can also be considered to be affected by sociocultural factors, in addition to being a test of common sense. In general, the information, vocabulary, and comprehension subtests show the least change after diffuse brain damage and, further, are not often useful in shedding light on the nature of a learning disability. The similarities subtest is a good measure of verbal reasoning, requiring the child to determine the similarity between objects. Of all of the verbal subtests, the arithmetic and digit span subtests usually get the most attention from clinicians. The digit span consists of a forward and backward digit span and is sensitive to disorders of short-term memory, sequencing, and mental rotation. Denckla and Rudel (1974) suggested that differences between groups of learning-disabled children (for instance, auditory and visual dyslexics) may be reflected in disparities between the two portions of the digit span, which are usually performed using different strategies. The arithmetic subtest of the WISC-R is also a complex measure of several intellectual functions (including the obvious, the ability to carry out arithmetic problems). The test is administered orally and requires good concentration, auditory memory, reasoning, and, because the test is timed, speed of calculation.

In contradistinction to the verbal scale, the performance scale subtests require visual analysis and, in all but one subtest, a manual response. Because many children with learning disabilities also suffer from motor dyscoordination, they often score very poorly on the performance subtests. These results are sometimes mistakenly viewed as "visual perceptual problems." It is important, therefore, to determine the contribution of any motor-executional deficit before concluding that the problem is one of a visual perceptual processing nature.

The digit symbol test is often a very troublesome task for learning-disabled children because it requires rapid number-symbol transcoding. Children with graphomotor and visual-spatial orientation difficulties can be expected to perform very poorly on this timed test. The picture completion test is a measure of visual reasoning ability, requiring the subject to find missing parts of common objects and make a verbal response. The block design subtest is a visuoconstructive task calling upon the child to copy a design set forth by the examiner. Since the task requires spatial organization ability, children with directional difficulties perform very poorly on this subtest. Object assembly and picture arrangement are tests of visual organization and conceptual reasoning. Both are timed tests and thus reward subjects who are facile with visual problems and are rapid in completing the manual response. The coding subtest is a test of visuoconstructive ability-maze solution for children under eight and design reproduction for older children.

Other tests of general intellectual ability may be substituted for the WISC-R, although few will provide as comprehensive an analysis of mental function as the Wechsler test. The Stanford-Binet Intelligence Scale (Terman and Merrill 1960) measures a myriad of different verbal abilities but is generally considered to be weak in the assessment of nonverbal functions. Raven's Coloured Progressive Matrices (Raven 1962) and Standard Progressive Matrices (Raven 1958) are tests of general intellectual ability and visual pattern matching. A considerable amount of neuropsychological research has been done with the Raven tests (Archibald et al. 1967; Costa 1976; Zaidel and Sperry 1977) with conflicting results as to what the test measures. It can be concluded, however, that the tests are much more appropriate as visual-spatial reasoning tests than tests of general intelligence.

Numerous brief screening tests exist that have some applicability in separating out intellectually deficient children from those who may have specific learning disabilities. One such test that is widely used with school children is the Slosson Intelligence Test for Children and Adults (Slosson 1963).

LANGUAGE TESTS

The assessment of language functions plays a very important role in children with learning problems. Quite clearly, school success is dependent upon linguistic ability. The explanation of the interrelationship between speech and reading problems in dyslexic children was an early contribution of Orton (1925, 1937) but the precise nature of this interrelationship remains to be specified. Language disorders are relative in severity (sometimes the term "dysphasia" is substituted for "aphasia" by some clinicians) and often involve more than one area of difficulty (such as articulation). Thorough language assessments should therefore include tests of speech comprehension, reading comprehension, articulation and verbal expression, oral reading, writing, spelling, and naming. Intensive examination should determine whether, for instance, an articulation disorder is a symptom of weak or spastic speech musculature (dysarthria), a symptom of an apraxia of speech, or a symptom of expressive aphasia.

Much information about a subject's language ability can be gleaned from conversational and expository speech (Goodglass and Kaplan 1972) or other informal testing techniques. The most frequently used general language tests are the IQ measures, but several aphasia examinations have been employed as screening tests for language disorders and also as measures of normal language development. The Halstead-Wepman Aphasia Test (Halstead and Wepman 1959), with its many modifications, is the most popular method for examining for aphasia. Other aphasia tests that have been successfully used with children include the Token Test (DeRenzi and Vignolo 1962), Boston Diagnostic Aphasia Test (Goodglass and Kaplan 1972), and the Neurosensory Center Comprehensive Examination for Aphasia (Spreen and Benton 1969). Other tests of linguistic function that have been shown to be very sensitive to the effects of brain damage and subtle language disorders (such as agrammatism) include the Test of Syntactic Comprehension (Parisi and Pizzamiglio 1970), the Syntax Token Test (Dennis and Kohn 1975), and the Semantic Anomalies Test (Dennis and Whitaker 1976).

Agrammatism has been found to be an important deficit in expressive aphasia (Whitaker 1971), left hemispherectomy for infantile hemiplegia (Dennis and Whitaker 1976), left temporal lobe agenesis (Pirozzolo et al. 1977b; Pirozzolo et al. 1978), and auditory-linguistic dyslexia (Pirozzolo et al. 1977a). In addition to the tests previously mentioned, the Northwestern Syntax Test (Lee 1969) and Grammatic Closure Test of the ITPA have been used with some success in this regard.

Anomic aphasics and auditory-linguistic dyslexics are deficient in word-finding ability, perhaps the most neglected and least understood language process. The Naming Fluency, Visual Confrontation Naming, and Responsive Naming subtests of the Boston Diagnostic Aphasia Test adequately tap the complexity of the naming process. The naming function is exceedingly important, as pointed out by Mattis et al. (1975), who have argued that it is the most predominant deficit in a language disorder type of dyslexia.

Perhaps the best method of assessing expressive language ability, which has been virtually ignored (Wepman, personal communication), may be the neurolinguistic analysis of responses to the Thematic Apperception Technique (Murray, 1938), a projective personality test. This method circumvents problems surrounding the objective tests and gives a more accurate, naturalistic, and valid example of a subject's language corpus.

Another popular measure of language comprehension is the Peabody Picture Vocabulary Test (Dunn 1965). It has been used in a considerable amount of neuropsychological research (for example,

Zaidel 1976) and is very useful in determining the language comprehension of expressive aphasics and children with speech disorders because it does not require a verbal response. The child points to a picture that is a symbol of the concept described by the examiner from the test protocol.

A number of adequate measures of reading comprehension exist. The Wide Range Achievement Test (Jastak and Jastak 1965) contains a reading phase that is a highly inaccurate measure of reading fluency but yet a good test of word recognition or decoding. The Gray Oral Reading Test (Gray 1959) enables an examiner to determine oral reading (decoding) grade level and a reading comprehension level. Many other reading tests have subtests that purport to measure the strength of various reading skills such as decoding, silent reading comprehension, text comprehension, and so on.

Although no formal technique is necessary for the assessment of spelling ability, good norms are available on the spelling phase of the Wide Range Achievement Test. This instrument is probably the most commonly used in the assessment of spelling grade level in neuropsychology because it is easily administered and provides normative information.

PERCEPTUAL TESTS

Wepman speculated that learning disabilities result from one or more disorders of the following functions: auditory discrimination, auditory sequencing, auditory memory, visual discrimination, visual sequencing, visual memory, and spatial ability. The notion that learning disabilities have a perceptual basis is very compelling and has led to the development of several test batteries based on this model. The Illinois Test of Psycholinguistic Abilities (ITPA, Kirk et al. 1968) is probably the most popular single instrument used in the assessment of learning disabilities. Somewhat similar to the Wechsler Scales, it consists of two groups (channels) of subtests: auditory-vocal and visual-motor. In addition to measures of perceptual discrimination, sequencing, and memory, the ITPA also contains tests of language expression, grammar, and phonemic abilities. As with the WISC-R, large discrepancies in performance between the auditory-vocal and visual-motor channel subtests are thought to reveal basic perceptual processing disturbances (Pirozzolo and Hess 1976).

Wepman and his associates have designed original tests of auditory discrimination (Wepman 1958), auditory memory span (Wepman and Morency 1973), auditory sequencing (Wepman and Morency 1975), visual discrimination (Wepman et al. 1975b), visual memory (Wepman et al. 1975a), and spatial orientation memory (Wepman and Turaids 1975). The Auditory Discrimination Test is the oldest and most well-known test of phonemic discrimination and is widely used with brain-damaged, learning-disabled, and normal populations. Preliminary evidence suggests that the remainder of the Wepman battery of perceptual tests will be helpful in delineating the causes of retarded reading.

Face recognition is an important perceptual-processing ability that some developmental dyslexics appear to lack (Pontius 1976), although it is unclear as to how this ability relates to reading acquisition. Benton and Van Allen (1973) have designed the most widely used clinical test of face recognition. Although most evidence would suggest that dyslexics have good face recognition ability (Marcel and Rajan 1975; Pirozzolo and Rayner 1979), more research is clearly indicated to determine whether disabled readers with visual-spatial processing problems have symptoms of prosopagnosia.

TESTS OF MOTOR ABILITY AND PERCEPTUAL MOTOR INTEGRATION

The role of oculomotor scanning ability in information processing has been the subject of much study (see, for example, Luria 1966). Numerous methods can be employed to determine a reader's ability to perform voluntary saccadic eye movements including electrooculographic or infrared pupil-tracking techniques. Although these methods are not always available or convenient, several screening tests exist that will provide adequate information about saccadic eye movements and their role in visual perception. Such methods include Rey's Tangled Lines Test (1964) and its subsequent modifications (Selnes 1977; Pirozzolo 1977b), or any of the various visual-tracking techniques.

The excellent work of Satz and Friel (1974) has shown that tests for finger agnosia may be among the most reliable devices for predicting reading failure. There are, of course, many studies supporting this theory by showing a strong relationship between finger agnosia and reading disability (Hermann and Norrie 1958; Kinsbourne and Warrington 1963; Pirozzolo and Rayner 1978b). Tests for finger agnosia, three of which are described by Kinsbourne and Warrington (1962), reveal disturbances of body scheme, directionality, and tactile perception. Finger Tip Writing (Russell et al. 1970) or palm-writing (Rey 1964) techniques may also be performed to assess the child's tactile recognition, although finger agnosia tests are generally preferred with children who may not have learned basic arithmetic skills. Tests for astereognosis complete the series of tactile perception measures. These tests require a child to recognize several common objects by touch alone. Objects typically used include a key, pencil, coin, and paper clip.

The Visual Motor Gestalt Test (Bender 1938) occupies a place in almost every mental examination. It was devised to study the psychological development of children but is useful in assessing mental functions other than those that are of concern here. The reproduction of the nine geometric designs can reveal problems in visual discrimination and orientation or in the motor act of copying the figures. Brain-damaged patients with left hemisphere lesions resulting in apraxia draw highly simplified versions of the Bender forms, whereas patients with right hemisphere lesions resulting in visual-spatial agnosia draw spatially and directionally disorganized versions of the figures. As previously suggested, care must be taken not to infer causality from failure on this task. In order to separate out the visual perceptual component, Benton's Visual Retention Test (Benton 1963) or the Memory for Designs Test (Graham and Kendall 1960) may be added to the battery.

Screening tests for motor integration disorders may be especially important in the assessment of children with learning disorders. Reports of delays in cerebellar function in these children are numerous and thus several quick screening tests should be performed when dysmetria is suspected. Finger-to-nose, heel-to-knee, and rapid alternating opposition of the fingers with the thumb are simple cerebellar tests that can be performed without instrumentation. Higher motor abilities can be assessed by asking the child to perform various learned motor acts, such as how to use scissors, comb, toothbrush, hammer, and the like. The Purdue Pegboard Test (Purdue Research Foundation 1948) is a test of manual dexterity and speed that can be used in conjunction with a finger-tapping test and the aforementioned techniques to supply a complete measurement of motor integration.

6 CASE STUDIES

In the preceding chapters an attempt was made to characterize discrete forms of developmental dyslexia. In this chapter case studies are presented to illustrate the pattern of neuropsychological findings in these disorders. Serial studies of these groups have indicated that auditory-linguistic dyslexics have a psychometric profile that includes lower scores on auditory-verbal tests (for example, lower verbal than performance IQs, lower auditory-vocal than visual-motor ITPA scores). Their histories often reveal that they were later in acquiring speech and language skills than their siblings. Their reading and writing contains errors that predominantly involve the sight-sound relationships of letters and words. From a linguistic standpoint, errors often involve grammatical function words (as opposed to content words). In general, reading is a slow, laborious process because of faulty decoding skills. During informal testing one of the most striking disabilities that can be observed is a problem in short-term verbal memory when these children are asked to follow a series of directions (such as open the door, then pick up your pencil, then put the penny under the paper, then stand behind your chair). Auditory-linguistic dyslexics typically remember fewer of the commands than normals (or visual-spatial dyslexics) and further make a greater number of errors that involve the grammatical words of the commands (substituting "in front of" for behind or "next to" for under).

Charcot found that acquired dyslexics can relearn reading skills by using an alternative strategy to the decoding (sight-sound) approach. Remediation involves a method that evokes the auditory images of a word through the use of the tactile or kinesthetic sense, thus deemphasizing the visual stage. Examples of this method include the use of sandpaper letters and the use of kinesthetic cues such as writing on the palms of the hands. This approach to remedial reading generally fails as completely as the decoding method because it stresses the importance of the skills that auditory-linguistic dyslexics lack. As Mattis and his colleagues (1975) point out, the use of phonics serves only to frustrate the child with this form of reading disability. The most successful approach appears to be the method that bypasses phonology, namely, the "whole word" or "sight word" approach, which emphasizes the visual analysis of words and the connection between the orthographic features of text and the meaning of specific configurations of visual features. One delimitation would appear to be the fact that this approach, although it works well for children with supranormal compensatory intellectual abilities, is often a less than optimal strategy for teaching reading to children of subnormal or even normal intellectual ability.

Serial studies of visual-spatial dyslexics have demonstrated that these children have deficiencies in visuoconstructive ability and spatial relations. They have little directional awareness, often confusing left and right, and less frequently up and down. Psychometric profiles of visual-spatial dyslexics show that they are poor in visual-motor coordination, scoring more poorly on performance than verbal IQ subtests and more poorly on the visual-motor channel subtests than the auditory-vocal ITPA subtests. Other behavioral deficits include disorders of body schema, finger agnosia, and spatial dyscalculia. Reversals and letter confusions continue to be a source of reading difficulty long beyond the stage when these paralexias disappear in normal readers. Visual-spatial dyslexics may not be able to take advantage of parafoveal and peripheral cues in reading to the extent that fluent readers may. In addition to their characteristic deficiency in analyzing the visual features of text, they may also be constrained by functionally constricted visual fields.

Visual-spatial dyslexics lack an extensive "sight vocabulary" and read even some high-frequency words as though they are unfamiliar. On a standardized test of visual imagery, they are far inferior to normals and auditory-linguistic dyslexics in the amount of visual imagery they introduce into pictures they are asked to draw and stories they are asked to tell (Pirozzolo and Pirozzolo 1978). Remedial reading with these children usually stresses a linguistic approach, emphasizing the phonics method. Alternative methods such as the auditory-kinesthetic approach have also been successful in certain cases.

Two lines of inquiry exist in the behavioral sciences: the idiographic and nomothetic methods. Serial studies, which are currently the most popular in modern psychology, allow scientists to generalize beyond a specific population of subjects. Although the nomothetic is clearly the most popular method of inquiry, it inherently misses a great deal of information by its insistence upon the statistical average. The idiographic or case study method has provided science with perhaps the most salient behavioral data. The case study work of Freud and Piaget in the psychological sciences and the work of virtually all of the modern behavioral neurologists has advanced the behavioral sciences dramatically. The following two case studies of auditory-linguistic dyslexia and visual-spatial dyslexia, respectively, are presented with the notion in mind that studies of dyslexia that find the syndrome to be a fuzzy, undifferentiated catch-all clinical term have not recognized that true neuropsychological syndromes of developmental dyslexia characterized by interrelated clusters of symptoms may exist when dyslexics come under close neuropsychological scrutiny.

It has been shown that developmental dyslexia is often characterized by maturational lags or deficits at the highest levels of central nervous system functioning, which can include language disorders, visual-spatial agnosias, oculomotor scanning deficiencies, and problems with tactile perception. The following is a neuropsychological case study of auditory-linguistic dyslexia, which is characterized by symptoms relating to a central language system disorder. A diagnostic battery of neuropsychological, neurosensory, and neurolinguistic tests, including psychometric and educational tests assessing cognitive and perceptual functioning, a tachistoscopic recognition task, and a finger-tapping test, were administered to our subject. In addition, the subject's eye movements were recorded during reading.

Results of these tests suggest that language functions are impaired in auditory-linguistic dyslexia whereas visual-spatial functions remain intact. Oculomotor scanning does not appear to be impaired as indicated by the eye movement pattern during reading. It is hypothesized that the cerebral dysfunction involved affects the linguistic processes in reading while sparing others such as oculomotor and visual perceptual skills.

Skilled reading is clearly a multistage process that involves the transformation of orthographic featural information into a linguistic code. Because the left cerebral hemisphere is recognized as the cerebral substrate that governs verbal behavior, it is often supposed that reading acquisition is dependent only upon the special abilities of the left hemisphere. Despite this assumption, the results of several neuropsychological experiments discussed previously have provided evidence in favor of the hypothesis that both linguistic and visual-spatial abilities play an important role in the reading process and that this is especially true in beginning and backward reading. The objective of the case study to follow is to show that the initial stage of the reading process (the stage of visual analysis) can be intact in a dyslexic who manifests problems with the later stages of the reading process.

A 21-year-old high school graduate came to our attention as an example of an auditory-linguistic dyslexic. Interviews with him and his girlfriend (who referred him to us) suggested that his reading problem was not the result of inadequate cultural or social stimulation and that he had had adequate motivation to learn to read. This particular dyslexic was the subject of a previous communication (Pirozzolo et al. 1977a). He was self-employed as an automobile mechanic. He had several times previously been enrolled in tutorial programs for remedial reading, but each time he had dropped out because he was not satisfied with his progress. He learned to perform the duties of his profession by trial and error, virtually never reading instructions found in maintenance manuals. He reported that he was always good at working with his hands and solving intricate visual-spatial problems, a pattern commonly associated with auditory-linguistic dyslexia. Both the subject and his mother recall that his reading difficulty began in the first grade and that he got progressively further behind his classmates in reading. Medical and developmental histories were noncontributory, except for the fact that he was slower in acquiring spoken language than his siblings.

A number of tests traditionally employed with neurological patients was administered to our subject (B.T.) and the results are summarized in Table 6.1. His scores on the Wechsler Adult Intelligence Scale and Raven Standard Progressive Matrices indicated that he had age-appropriate-level intellectual ability. Results of the Wide Range Achievement Reading Test indicated that his word recognition skills were approximately at the fifth grade level. Other reading skills, such as those assessed by the Gray Oral Reading Test, suggested an even lower comprehension level. Many words beyond monosyllabic length gave him considerable difficulty in pronunciation and comprehension. Thus, although B.T. had normal intelligence, his reading performance was considerably retarded.

Other tests in the battery indicated that he had superior spatial abilities. His scores on the Money Road Map Test, Trail Making Test, and the performance scale subtests of the WAIS were all above average. Finger recognition and object recognition by touch were perfectly executed. A finger-tapping test including both unimanual and bimanual tasks showed that he had good speed and manual performance. However, using a design set forth by Kinsbourne and McMurray (1975) involving simultaneous verbal task execution (naming automobiles) and finger tapping, B.T.'s performance was significantly impaired for the right hand (contralateral

TABLE 6.1

Neuropsychological Test Results: B.T.

Test	Score	Test	Score
Wechsler Adult Intelligence Scale		Wepman Auditory Discrimination Test	
Verbal IQ	97		no errors
Performance IQ	114	Trail Making Test	
Raven Coloured Progressive Matrices		Trails A	17 s
		Trails B	45 s
WAIS equivalent	100	Money Road Map Test	
Wide Range Achievement Test			one error
Reading grade equivalent	4.7		
Arithmetic grade equivalent	6.7		
Spelling grade equivalent	5.7		

Tachistoscopic Recognition of Words Presented to the Left and Right Visual Fields

	B.T.	Controls (N = 10)
Threshold for unilateral word presentations	15 ms	28.5 ms
Words correct in right visual field	5	8
Words correct in left visual field	5	4.5
Visual confusions	4	6
Acoustic confusions	8	4
Foils	2	2.5
Threshold for bilateral word presentations	20 ms	44 ms
Words correct in right visual field	5	8
Words correct in left visual field	7	4
Visual confusions	8	6
Acoustic confusions	4	4
Foils	2	0

Source: Compiled by the author.

to the presumed language hemisphere). Table 6.2 shows the results of this experimental technique. In young children and in individuals whose verbal faculties are operating at less than optimal levels, one might expect that the overloading on this task would cause a marked performance deficit by the hand contralateral to the language hemisphere (Luria 1966).

TABLE 6.2

Finger-Tapping Test Results

Normal Condition: Uninterfered		Interference Condition: Naming	
Right hand	5.87/s	Right hand	4.98/s
Left hand	4.86/s	verbal output	11 names
		Left hand	5.28/s
		verbal output	29 names

Source: Compiled by the author.

A number of recent experiments, including those discussed previously, have employed a task utilizing tachistoscopic presentations of words displaced to the left and right of fixation in an attempt to specify possible anomalies of lateral specialization of the cerebral hemispheres in reading disability (see, for example, Marcel et al. 1974). Briefly, in normal adults and children, more words are recognized in the right visual field, presumably because it has more direct anatomical connections with the language mechanisms of the left hemisphere and transmission is not delayed by crossing the corpus callosum. In support of the notion that auditory-linguistic dyslexics suffer from a cerebral dysfunction in the language-dominant hemisphere, evidence was presented in Chapter 4 showing that these poor readers did not show the normal pattern of left hemisphere-right visual field superiority for word recognition. Auditory-linguistic dyslexics in this study as well as others showed no asymmetry in word recognition.

B.T. was presented with stimulus materials in a tachistoscopic word recognition task much like that used in the studies reported in Chapter 4. The stimulus materials were recently used in a study by Pirozzolo and Rayner (1977) with normal adult subjects.

Words were presented displaced by one degree and 41 minutes to the left or right of a central fixation point. Threshold durations were found for each condition in the unilateral and bilateral experiment. After each presentation the subject looked out of the tachistoscope and made a forced choice response concerning the word presented. The four response alternatives varied in terms of their similarity to each other. For example, if the subject was shown the word must in the tachistoscope, one of the responses was acoustically similar (dust), one was visually similar in that it had the same first letter and overall word shape as the target word (mark), and one was a foil (dark). The sets of words (must, dust, mark, dark) were all high-frequency words and could be used interchangeably so that if another word was the target, the remaining words fulfilled the requirements of the task in containing visually confusable, acoustically confusable, and foil items. Words were projected unilaterally and bilaterally. In the unilateral condition words projected to the right of fixation began at one degree 41 minutes, to the right of fixation and subtended two additional degrees of visual angle. When words were projected to the left they began at three degrees and 41 minutes and ended one degree and 41 minutes from the fixation point, thus subtending two degrees of visual angle. Table 6.1 shows B. T. 's performance as well as the mean performance from the Pirozzolo and Rayner (1977) study.

It should be noted that in relation to normal subjects B. T. was able to recognize words that were presented at very short threshold durations. This suggests that the initial visual perceptual processing of words is not related to the subject's dyslexia because this stage seems to be carried out well by B. T. In fact, it could be contended that this low-threshold exposure duration is further evidence of B. T. 's superior visual-perceptual-processing ability. When words were presented unilaterally, B. T. did not show the commonly observed left hemisphere-right visual field superiority. When words were presented bilaterally--a condition that usually results in an even more robust right visual field advantage--he showed a small right hemisphere-left visual field superiority. In addition, whereas the normal subjects made most of their errors on visually confusable alternatives, B. T. made more acoustically confusable errors. These observations support the underlateralization notion of Orton. Further, they give support to the notion that the perceptual systems (visual and auditory) are not synchronous in their development and that continued preferential use of the better differentiated system results in a modality preference (Wepman 1960). This preference is a cognitive style that should be detectable as a deficit where task requirements and cognitive style are incompatible, as with B. T. 's abnormal right hemisphere-left visual field superiority in word recognition. We must be cautious, however, not to infer laterality of language from this visual half-field experiment, that is, we should refrain from suggesting that a left visual field advantage indicates that language in this subject is lateralized in the right hemisphere (see Satz 1976 for a discussion of inferences that can be made from laterality tests). The finding of a left visual field advantage for word recognition may indicate that language processes are organized differently in this subject and the additional results may suggest that the dysfunction lies in the auditory system (a result that would be supported by the other data collected here).

EYE MOVEMENTS DURING READING

The eye movements of our subject were monitored in the same fashion as in the previously described studies, that is, by a Biometrics Model 200-1 eye movement monitor and a strip chart recorder as the subject read from Form B of the Gray Oral Reading Test. The comprehension questions accompanying Form B were administered following each passage and B. T. 's performance was comparable to his performance on Form A, which was used to determine his reading ability during the neuropsychological testing. Figure 6.1 shows the eye movement pattern of a graduate student of the same age reading passage B-9 (a), as well as B. T. 's eye movements reading passages B-3 (b), B-8 (c), and B-9 (d). B-3 and B-9 represent silent reading and B-8 represents oral reading.

There are a number of interesting observations that can be made from an examination of Figure 6.1, as well as the complete record of eye movements. First, when B. T. read passages that gave him little difficulty decoding and did not include words with which he was unfamiliar (B-3, for example), his eye movement pattern was not unlike that generally found among skilled readers. A simple comparison of B. T. 's eye movement pattern while reading B-3 and our graduate student's eye movements while reading B-9 indicates that they are very much alike. The number of fixations per line and the approximate duration of fixations are quite similar. Also, the number of regressions for both readers is around 10-20 percent, which is similar to the frequency of regressions reported by Spragins et al. (1976) for skilled readers and similar also to those found in the study reported in Chapter 4. As the passages became increasingly more difficult, however, the number of regressions increased (as they do in normal readers when text difficulty is increased) from 20 percent of the saccades on passage B-3 to 40 percent on passage B-9. The increase in frequency of regressions was also paralleled by an increase in the number of fixations. Generally,

FIGURE 6.1

Reading Eye Movements (B.T.)

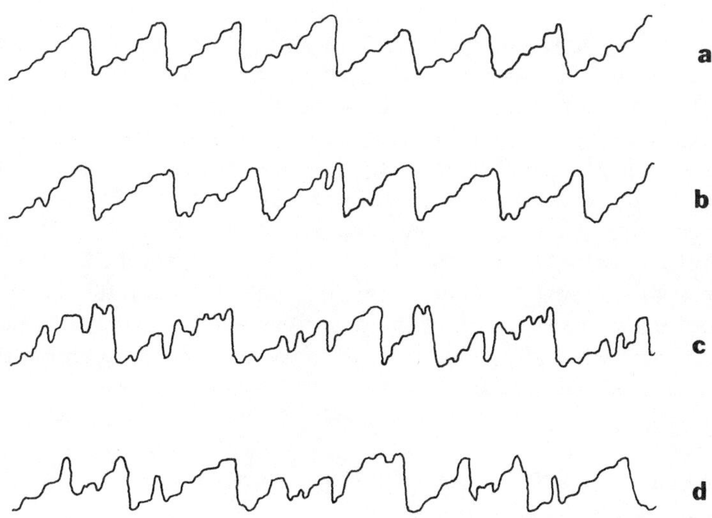

Source: F. J. Pirozzolo, K. Rayner, and H. A. Whitaker, "Left hemisphere mechanisms in dyslexia: A neuropsychological case study." International Neuropsychological Society (INS) presentation, 1977.

this increase in frequency of regressions and number of fixations can be accounted for by the same explanation. When B.T. encountered an unfamiliar word (in silent reading) or a word that he could not decode (oral reading), his strategy was to move ahead to the next word, regress to the word that preceded the unfamiliar word, look back at the unfamiliar word, and then start the cycle over again until he was able to interpret or decode the word. This strategy can be seen in Figure 6.1. Under oral reading conditions, the examiner marked in his scoring manual where the subject had difficulty decoding a word and this record was matched with the eye movement record. Under silent reading conditions, the examiner noted which lines yielded an abnormal eye movement pattern and, following the test administration, interviewed the subject in order to find out which words he had difficulty understanding. In addition to using the strategy of using the context to understand or decode a difficult word, B.T. also made a series of very short saccades within the difficult word. In attempting to understand or decode the word, the subject adopted an almost letter-by-letter strategy, which is characteristic of children who are just learning to read. By fixating the word prior to and following a difficult word, B.T. was obviously trying to understand it by relying on the context to provide clues to meaning.

It is plausible, therefore, to suggest that B.T.'s reading problems are not due to faulty eye movements. Although visual-spatial dyslexics can be expected to show oculomotor scanning deficiencies such as a large proportion of right-to-left saccades, B.T.'s eye movement pattern did not show these anomalies. As long as the reading material presented him was not difficult, his eye movement pattern was normal in every respect. As the text became more difficult, he relied on words prior to and following a difficult word as clues to meaning (and decoding), and as more difficult words led to shorter saccades, his fixation durations and frequency of regressions increased markedly, yielding eye movement patterns unlike that found in skilled readers.

A NEUROLINGUISTIC ANALYSIS OF READING AND WRITING PERFORMANCE

A linguistic analysis of errors made during a modified administration of Form A of the Gray Oral Reading Test was done from an audiotape recording (it was this administration that was used in determining the subject's reading grade level). B.T. made 81 paralexic errors at his reading level. There were over two times as many errors of grammatical function or categorization (58 total errors) as there were errors of the major lexical items, noun, verb, adjective, and adverb (23 total errors). The errors of grammatical function or categorization involved tense, auxiliary verbs, articles, semantically weak prepositions, conjunctions, comparative and possessive inflections, relative and personal pronouns, number agreements, and changes of grammatical category. This analysis showed a clear agrammatic character to B.T.'s dyslexic reading.

His writing ability was further developed than his reading, although a few of the same kinds of errors were manifested. Writing to dictation was marked by a large number of phoneme-to-grapheme correspondence errors ("missile" as "missle," "judging" as "juging," "butcher" as "bousher," and "knuckle" as "nakel," for example). There was no specificity of word type for these errors; similar errors occurred on colors, body parts, function words, and arbitrarily chosen lexical items. When he was asked to spontaneously write an essay describing his work, his written production contained very little punctuation, simple phrases, and no clear sentence structure.

He did, however, make use of some prepositions, conjunctions, and articles.

Errors of sequencing, either letters and phonemes at the word level, or words at the sentence level, were not prominent in his performance. This is in contrast to the performance seen in visual-spatial dyslexia. Listening comprehension as measured by additional reading tests showed good understanding of the text.

This subject appears to be a good clinical model of auditory-linguistic dyslexia. Psychometrically, the large verbal-performance discrepancy may suggest specific difficulties with the left hemisphere language processing. Success on the performance scale (and other measures of visual-spatial ability) suggests an intact, well-differentiated visual-spatial system in the posterior left and right hemispheres, although weaker performance on verbal tasks and agrammatism might be attributable to a left hemisphere language dysfunction. Further studies, such as those involving computerized tomography, evoked potentials, and regional cerebral blood flow, will be carried out to determine the intertest reliability of our measures.

VISUAL-SPATIAL DYSLEXIA

The following is a case study of a patient who was referred because she had an unusual handwriting orientation and because she had great difficulty reproducing geometric drawings in their proper spatial relationship. Although she was a college student, her reading level was equivalent to that of a sixth grade student. Neuropsychological testing showed that she had normal range verbal abilities. Severe deficits in spatial function, directional orientation, finger differentiation, calculational ability, and copying were also found. Using the infrared pupil-tracking technique described previously, we monitored the horizontal saccades of this patient while reading from the Gray Oral Reading Test. Fixation durations were normal but instances of reverse staircase movement were exhibited in several places in the record. The processing of spatial information in this patient was severely disturbed and this probably accounted for the abnormal scanning--an "irrepressible tendency" to move her eyes in a right-to-left direction. Because of her problems in directional orientation, finger differentiation, copying, and mathematics, the term "developmental Gerstmann syndrome" was used to describe her disorder. She also was the subject of a previous communication (Pirozzolo and Rayner 1978b).

The developmental Gerstmann syndrome is clinically characterized by finger agnosia, directional disorientation, dysgraphia, and dyscalculia (Kinsbourne and Warrington 1965; Benson and

Geschwind 1970; Pirozzolo and Rayner 1978b), and frequently occurs in children with developmental dyslexia. Hermann and Norrie (1958) were the first to recognize that some dyslexic children bore a similarity to adults with lesions involving the left inferior parietal lobe (angular gyrus).

Although there continues to be a dispute as to whether the Gerstmann syndrome actually represents a true clinical entity (see Benton 1977, and Gardner 1975, for reviews), patients with the full syndrome of deficits (finger agnosia, directional disorientation, dysgraphia, and dyscalculia) more often than not have lesions in the left angular gyrus. We have used the developmental construct, first used by Kinsbourne and Warrington, to suggest that the disorders of higher cortical function that occur in the controversial syndrome exist in our patient and that there is an absence of other focal neurological signs.

There has recently been a revival of interest in writing posture, a fact due, in part, to the attention attracted to the work of Levy and Reid (1976). Very few adequate explanations for abnormal handwriting orientations exist despite this revival of interest and the fact that these disorders were once the subject of much study (Hotz 1900; Critchley 1928; Benson 1970). Very few cases have been studied carefully and only Benson has offered a plausible explanation for the disorders.

The patient was a left-handed 22-year-old college student who was referred for neurological and neuropsychological evaluation because of extreme difficulty with reading and writing. Except for problems with directionality, calculation, reading, and writing, her development appears to have been relatively normal. She was born in January of 1955 to a mother who has reported having an ovarian tumor operation during pregnancy. Delivery and postnatal periods were normal.

On examination at 21 years, she showed corrected 20/25 visual acuity in both eyes. Her head circumference (occipitofrontal) was only 53 centimeters, which is in the third percentile for a 15-year-old girl. Her auditory acuity was within normal limits. She could hear a whispered voice from six feet on either side of her head. Further examination of cranial nerves revealed that they were all intact. Examination of motor function showed normal strength, tone, and reflexes with no evidence of cerebellar disorder. Finger recognition assessment using the three tests described by Kinsbourne and Warrington (1962) showed extremely hesitant, faulty finger differentiation.

The patient reported that she had always had great difficulty with spatial relations, reading, and writing. She remembered that it was easier for her to read upside down when she was learning to read but that her third grade teacher forced her to read in the normal orientation. Since that time she has read (laboriously) with text in the normal orientation. Her normal writing style is to start at the bottom of the page writing right to left, upside down, and up the page so that the opposing observer can readily read it (see Figure 6.2). Although her drawings are internally correct, the same style persists, and the drawings are inverted.

She becomes very confused about spatial relationships and directionality in unfamiliar settings. She relies on verbal labels wherever possible to find her way around even the most familiar surroundings. She becomes easily frustrated when requested to carry out commands such as, "Show me your left ring finger with your right index finger." She is unable to establish directional orientation readily enough to follow even simple commands.

FIGURE 6.2

Handwriting Orientation (C.B.)

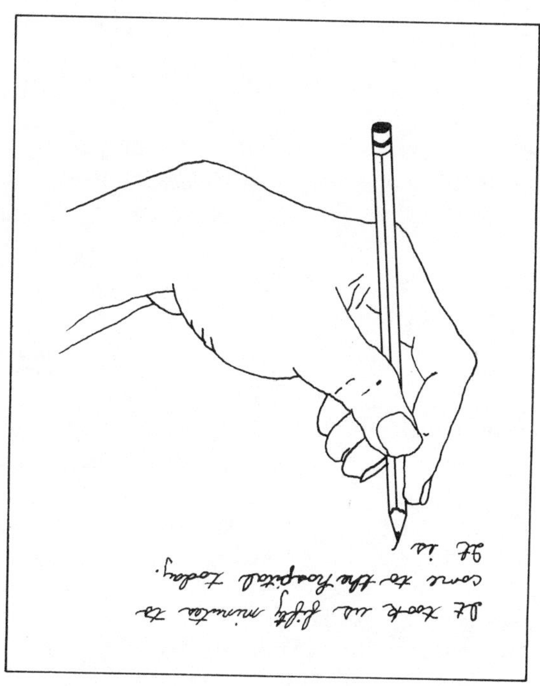

Source: F. J. Pirozzolo and K. Rayner, Brain and Language, Vol. 5 (New York: Academic Press, 1978b), p. 121.

NEUROPSYCHOLOGICAL EXAMINATION

Oral expressive language is grossly normal in this patient during expository and conversational speech. As her academic background would suggest, she is functionally within the average intellectual range, scoring a full-scale WAIS IQ of 102, with a six-point discrepancy between the verbal and performance scales (in favor of the verbal). Table 6.3 shows the results of this testing.

TABLE 6.3

Neuropsychological Test Results: C.B.

Wechsler Adult Intelligence Scale		Wepman Auditory Discrimination Test	no errors
Full-scale IQ	102	Spatial Orientation Memory Test	1st percentile
Verbal scale IQ	104	Gray Oral Reading Test	
Performance scale IQ	98	Grade equivalent	6th grade
Rey Visual Word Discrimination Test	10th percentile	Visual Half-Field Experiment	
Rey Tangled Lines Test	1st percentile	Threshold for recognizing unilaterally presented words	70 ms
Lady Walking in the Rain Test	1st percentile		

Source: Compiled by the author.

Visual-motor coordination was assessed by Benton's Visual Retention Test as normal, although each of the forms was reversed. On two clinical tests of oculomotor scanning ability (Rey 1964; Pirozzolo 1977b), she performed well below the first percentile on one and well below the tenth percentile on the other. The error pattern suggested that she could not make successive left-to-right saccades across the page of the test.

Reading comprehension level, as assessed by the Gray Oral Reading Test, suggested a sixth grade comprehension level. Error analysis again revealed a problem with lateral scanning. When she reached the end of a line of print she did not always know where to move her eyes to continue reading. Often she would move her eye down one or two lines and begin reading from right to left.

In the experimental tachistoscopic task used in the previous case study, her threshold exposure duration was greatly increased in all conditions, suggesting a basic visual-perceptual-processing defect.

READING EYE MOVEMENTS

Our subject's eye movements were monitored while she read from Form B of the Gray Oral Reading Test. Silent reading and oral reading were alternated between passages. Comprehension questions were administered after completion of the passages and performance was comparable to that on Form A. Figure 6.3 shows the eye movement pattern of a college student of the same age (P.H.) reading from the Gray Oral Reading Test (a), as well as samples of our subject's (C.B.) eye movement patterns. As can be seen in Figure 6.3 (c), C.B.'s eye movement pattern when reading text in the normal orientation often showed instances of right-to-left scanning. Note in particular the instance of successive right-to-left saccades after completion of a line. After three or four saccades toward the left, she corrected her pattern by moving to the left margin of the text and then began a series of left-to-right saccades. This pattern of eye movements was observable to the examiner because in oral reading C.B. would often complete a line and then begin reading the last words on the next line.

FIGURE 6.3

Reading Eye Movements (C.B.)

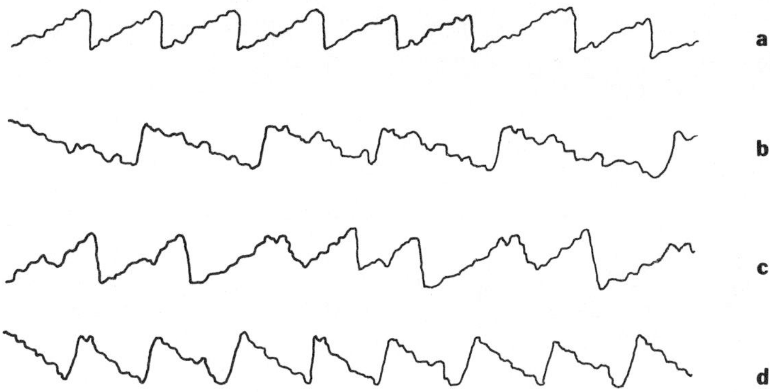

Source: F. J. Pirozzolo and K. Rayner, Brain and Language, Vol. 5 (New York: Academic Press, 1978b), p. 124.

Immediately after the session in which her eye movements were recorded while she was reading text in its normal orientation, we presented for her to read text that was inverted (upside down). Figure 6.3 shows that her eye movement pattern while reading inverted text (d) was of the staircase pattern that is typical of normal readers (except that the saccades are right to left instead of left to right). For comparison, we recorded the eye movements of our control subject (P. H.) while reading inverted text (b). Interestingly, reading comprehension improved to the tenth grade level in our subject when she was able to read inverted text, despite the fact that she had not read this way since third grade.

DISCUSSION

These results corroborate those of Gruber (1962) and Zangwill and Blakemore (1972), who suggested that the reverse staircase movement pattern and the inability to perform return sweeps in certain dyslexics were due to an "irrepressible tendency" to scan text in a right-to-left direction. Mosse and Daniels (1959) identified a syndrome of dyslexia that they termed linear dyslexia and in which the cardinal deficit was one of an inability to perform a return sweep. Ciuffreda et al. (1976) also reported a case of a dyslexic who had extreme difficulty making return sweeps and consequently made a large proportion of right-to-left saccades.

The patient reported here exhibits all of the symptoms of developmental Gerstmann syndrome, a severe spatial disability. She presented with an extreme form of visual-spatial dyslexia that is thought to result from disordered visual orientation. Her inverted writing can also be considered a symptom of an underlying spatial disorder. Taken together, the symptomatology would strongly point to a disturbance in the function of the left angular gyrus region, thought to be the site of the pathophysiology in developmental dyslexia since 1896 (Morgan 1896).

7 SUMMARY AND CONCLUSIONS

The purpose of this book was to examine the assumption that developmental dyslexia is characterized by certain cognitive deficits that may reflect a dysfunction in the way the brain handles incoming sensory information. Although there is little agreement as to the nature of the pathophysiology in dyslexia, there is some agreement that information processing is not as efficient or perhaps not as rapid as in the normal brain. In addition to theories about the role of neurotransmitters in the etiology of developmental dyslexia, two neuroanatomical observations lead to two other speculations about the causal factors in the syndrome. First, computerized transaxial tomography has been used to demonstrate certain structural asymmetries in the brain. Hier and his colleagues (1978) used the computerized transaxial scan procedure to show that there is a reversal of cerebral asymmetries in some dyslexic children. This observation would appear to be the first study of brain structure to support Orton's anomalous lateralization theory. Reading fluency may not develop then because the centers for language are not sufficiently developed to the required anatomical specifications. Studies of the regional development of the brain along quite a different line would lead to a second hypothesis about causal mechanisms. Yakovlev and Lecours (1967) demonstrated that the angular gyrus, the structure so uniquely important in reading, is among the last regions of the brain to reach anatomical maturity (as indicated by the end of the myelination cycle). The psychological deficit in developmental dyslexia is one of a decrease in efficiency and because myelin serves to speed the conduction of electrical impulses down axons and to insulate those axons from the "noise" of other neurons, it would seem reasonable to suggest that late myelination causes developmental dyslexia. This would also seem plausible because the "miraculous recoveries" sometimes seen around puberty roughly coincide with a suspected anatomical maturity in brain regions known to be important in reading.

Empirical research was presented in this book to test the hypothesis that independent neuropsychological syndromes of developmental dyslexia exist.

Two subgroups of developmental dyslexia were delineated from a large clinical population on the basis of behavioral descriptions, writing samples, neuropsychological and educational test results. One subgroup (auditory-linguistic dyslexics) had language disorder symptoms such as impaired language expression, lower verbal IQ, agrammatism, and faulty grapheme-to-phoneme matching in reading. The second subgroup (visual-spatial dyslexics) had weaknesses in visual, spatial, and oculomotor skills such as directional and topographical disorientation, spatial dysgraphia and dyscalculia, and finger agnosia.

Three tasks were designed to test the assumption that the two subgroups proposed should differ in their behavioral performance on measures of visual-information-processing ability. A foveal and parafoveal word recognition study demonstrated that normal children and visual-spatial dyslexics showed no lateral asymmetry. No differences between the groups exhibited a strong right visual field superiority, while auditory-linguistic dyslexics were observed when words were presented in foveal vision. Auditory-linguistic dyslexics' performance in the left visual field was highly similar to that of normals. Visual-spatial dyslexics were considerably poorer than normals at all parafoveal locations.

A saccadic reaction time study revealed that auditory-linguistic dyslexics and normal readers exhibited shorter latencies for rightward saccadic eye movements. Visual-spatial dyslexics showed the opposite asymmetry.

Strip chart recordings of reading eye movements indicated that the pattern of eye movements in auditory-linguistic dyslexics was similar to that of normal readers in fixation duration, fixation frequency, and regression frequency when text difficulty was carefully controlled. Visual-spatial dyslexics showed atypical reading eye movement patterns with many instances of faulty, right-to-left scanning and return sweep inaccuracies. The results strongly support the notion that at least two neurobehavioral syndromes of developmental dyslexia exist.

Auditory-linguistic dyslexics are impaired on tasks requiring rapid, complex linguistic processing and it was hypothesized that late maturation of the fiber pathways involved in these left hemisphere language functions is the causal factor in this form of dyslexia. Visual-spatial dyslexics are impaired on tasks requiring visual discrimination, analysis, and memory, and it was hypothesized that the late maturation of fiber pathways in the left hemisphere's visual association areas (and possibly the corpus callosum) is the causal factor in this form of dyslexia.

It has been shown that reading and reading disability have always been controversial topics in scientific circles. Reading is perhaps a more controversial issue now than ever before, but the site of the battleground has shifted in recent years. Reading has become a political issue. Educators, parents, and politicians argue the benefits of teaching reading skills (as opposed to teaching the content areas) and debate the important question of whether children should be allowed to graduate from high school without attaining a specified reading comprehension level.

Neuropsychological research has provided some very valuable scientific information about "why Johnny can't read." The name of science has been tarnished by pseudoscientists who claim that they can decrease the incidence of dyslexia by using a specific reading program, or teach a child to read by training him to crawl, or remediate any reading difficulty by using special instrumentation. The challenge for future research on the neuropsychology of developmental reading disorders is to determine the exact functional losses in reading disability and find some appropriate methods for working with individual children. Experience in the rehabilitation of brain-damaged patients has clearly shown that the most important factor is not the method but the patient's relationship with the therapist. The recognition that it is the psychological contact between teacher and student that is the basis for learning rather than the program or method is the most important practical message that neuropsychology has communicated.

BIBLIOGRAPHY

Alpern, H. P., and Greer, C. A. 1977. "A dopaminergic basis for the effects of amphetamine on a mouse 'preadolescent hyperkinetic' model." Life Sciences 21, 93-98.

Archibald, Y., Wepman, J. M., and Jones, L. V. 1967. "Performance on nonverbal cognitive tests following unilateral cortical injury to the right and left hemisphere." Journal of Nervous and Mental Disease 145, 25-36.

Baloh, R. W., and Honrubia, V. 1976. "Reaction time and accuracy of the saccadic eye movements of normal subjects in a moving-target task." Aviation, Space and Environmental Medicine 47, 1165-68.

Baloh, R. W., Kumley, W. E., and Honrubia, V. 1976. "Algorithm for analyses of saccadic eye movements using a digital computer." Aviation, Space and Environmental Medicine 47, 523-27.

Bartz, A. E. 1962. "Eye movement latency, duration and response time as a function of angular displacement." Journal of Experimental Psychology 64, 318-24.

Bayle, E. 1942. "The nature and causes of regressive movements in reading." Journal of Experimental Education 11, 16-36.

Beaumont, J. G. 1976. "The cerebral laterality of 'minimal brain damage' in children." Cortex 12, 373-82.

Bender, L. 1938. "A visual motor Gestalt test and its clinical use." American Ortho-Psychiatric Association Research Monographs No. 3.

Bender, M. 1959. Psychopathology of Children with Organic Brain Disorders. Springfield, Mass.: Charles C. Thomas.

Benson, D. F. 1970. "Graphic orientation disorders of left handed children." Journal of Learning Disabilities 3, 126-31.

Benson, D. F., and Geschwind, N. 1969. "The alexias." In Handbook of Clinical Neurology Vol. 4, edited by D. J. Vinken and G. W. Bruyn. Amsterdam: North Holland.

Benson, D. F., and Geschwind, N. 1970. "Developmental Gerstmann syndrome." Neurology 20, 293-98.

Benton, A. L. 1963. The Revised Visual Retention Test. New York: Psychological Corporation.

Benton, A. L. 1977. "Reflections on the Gerstmann syndrome." Brain and Language 4, 44-61.

Benton, A. L., and Joynt, R. J. 1960. "Early descriptions of aphasia." Archives of Neurology 3, 205-20.

Benton, A. L., and Van Allen, M. W. 1973. Test of Facial Recognition Manual. Neurosensory Center Publication No. 287. University of Iowa.

Berlucchi, G., Crea, F., DiStefano, M., and Tassarini, G. 1977. "Influence of spatial stimulus response compatibility on reaction time of ipsilateral and contralateral hand to lateralized light stimuli." Journal of Experimental Psychology (Human Perception and Performance) 3, 505-17.

Blake, M. B., and Dearborn, W. F. 1935. "The improvement of reading habits." Journal of Higher Education 6, 83-88.

Blanchard, P. 1946. "Psychoanalytic contributions to the problem of reading disabilities." Psychoanalytic Study of Children 2, 163-88.

Boder, E. 1971. "Developmental dyslexia: Prevailing diagnostic concepts and a new diagnostic approach." In Progress in Learning Disabilities, edited by H. Myklebust. New York: Grune and Stratton.

Boder, E. 1973. "Developmental dyslexia: A diagnostic approach based on three atypical reading-spelling patterns." Developmental Medicine and Child Neurology 15, 663-87.

Bogen, J., and Bogen, G. 1976. "Wernicke's region: Where is it?" In Origins and Evolution of Language and Speech, edited by S. Harnard, H. D. Steklis, and J. Lancaster. New York: New York Academy of Sciences.

Bouma, H. 1973. "Visual interference in the parafoveal recognition of initial and final letters of words." Vision Research 13, 767-82.

Bouma, H., and Legein, C. P. 1977. "Foveal and parafoveal recognition of letters and words by dyslexics and average readers." Neuropsychologia 15, 69-80.

Brase, D. A., and Loh, H. H. 1978. "Possible role of 5-hydroxytryptamine in minimal brain dysfunction." Life Sciences 16, 1005-16.

Broadbent, W. H. 1872. "On the cerebral mechanism of speech and thought." Medico-Chirurgical Transactions 55, 145-94.

Brown, J. 1972. Aphasia, Apraxia and Agnosia. Springfield, Mass.: Charles C. Thomas.

Buswell, G. T. 1922. Fundamental Reading Habits: A Study of Their Development. Supplement, Educational Monograph, no. 21.

Buxbaum, E. 1964. "The patients' role in etiology of learning disability." Psychoanalytical Study of Children 19, 421-77.

Cattell, J. M. 1885. "Ueber die Zeit der Erkennung und Bennenung von Schriftzeichen, Bildern und Farben." Philosophische Studien 2, 635-50.

Cattell, J. M. 1886. "The time it takes to see and name objects." Mind 11, 63-65.

Charcot, J. M. 1890. Oeuvres completes. Three volumes. Paris: Lecrosnier et Babe.

Ciuffreda, K. J., Bahill, A. T., Kenyon, R. V., and Stark, L. 1976. "Eye movements during reading: Case reports." American Journal of Optometry and Physiological Optics 53, 389-95.

Claiborne, J. H. 1906. "Types of congenital symbol amblyopia." Journal of the American Medical Association 47, 1813-16.

Cohen, M. E., and Ross, L.E. 1977. "Saccadic latency in children and adults: Effects of warning interval and target eccentricity." Journal of Experimental Child Psychology 16, 539-49.

Conant, L. F. 1964. "A study of eye movement behavior in reading performance of mature readers on reading selections of increased difficulty." Dissertation Abstracts 25, 7075-76.

Costa, L. D. 1976. "Interset variability on the Raven Coloured Progressive Matrices as an indicator of specific ability deficit in brain lesioned patients." Cortex 12, 31-40.

Critchley, M. 1928. Mirror Writing. London: Kegan Paul.

Critchley, M. 1970. The Dyslexic Child. London: Heinemann.

Dejerine, J. 1891. "Contribution a l'etude anatomopathologique cecite verbale." Memoires de la Societe de Biologie 4, 61-90.

Dejerine, J. 1892. "Des differentes varietes de cecite verbale." Memoires de la Societe de Biologie, Feb. 27, 1-30.

Delacato, C. 1963. The Diagnosis and Treatment of Speech and Reading Problems. Springfield, Mass.: Charles C. Thomas.

Denckla, M. B., and Rudel, R. 1974. "Rapid 'automatized' naming of pictured objects, colors, letters, and numbers by normal children." Cortex 10, 186-202.

Denckla, M. B., and Rudel, R. 1976. "Names of object-drawings by dyslexic and other learning disabled children." Brain and Language 3, 1-15.

Dennis, M., and Kohn, B. 1975. "Comprehension of syntax in infantile hemiplegics after cerebral hemidecortication: Left hemisphere superiority." Brain and Language 2, 472-82.

Dennis, M., and Whitaker, H. A. 1976. "Language acquisition following hemidecortication: Linguistic superiority of the left over the right hemisphere." Brain and Language 3, 404-33.

DeRenzi, E., and Vignolo, L. A. 1962. "The Token Test: A sensitive test to detect disturbances in aphasics." Brain 85, 665-78.

Doehring, D. G. 1968. Patterns of Impairment in Specific Reading Disability. Bloomington: Indiana University Press.

Dossetor, D. R., and Papaioannou, J. 1975. "Dyslexia and eye movements." Language and Speech 18, 312-17.

Drake, W. 1968. "Clinical and pathological findings in a child with a developmental learning disability." Journal of Learning Disabilities 1, 468-75.

Drew, A. 1956. "A neurological appraisal of familial congenital word blindness." Brain 79, 440-60.

Dunn, L. M. 1965. Expanded Manual for the Peabody Picture Vocabulary Test. Circle Pines, Minn.: American Guidance Service.

Eames, T. H. 1934. "The anatomical basis of lateral dominance anamolies." American Journal of Orthopsychiatry 4, 524-28.

Eames, T. H. 1935. "A frequency study of physical handicaps in reading disability and unselected groups." Journal of Educational Research 29, 1-5.

Eames, T. H. 1936. Restrictions of the visual fields as handicaps to learning." Journal of Educational Research 29, 460-65.

Eisenberg, L. 1966. "The epidemiology of reading retardation and a program for preventive intervention." In The Disabled Reader, edited by J. Money. Baltimore: Johns Hopkins.

Fedio, P., and Van Buren, J. 1974. "Memory deficits during electrical stimulation of the speech cortex in conscious man." Brain and Language 1, 29-42.

Feingold, B. F. 1975. Why Your Child is Hyperactive. New York: Random House.

Fisher, J. H. 1905. "A case of congenital word blindness (inability to learn to read)." Ophthalmological Review 24, 315.

Fisher, J. H. 1910. "Congenital word-blindness (inability to learn to read)." Transactions of the Ophthalmological Society of the United Kingdom 30, 216-25.

Flechsig, P. 1901. "Developmental (myelogenetic) localization of the cerebral cortex in the human subject." Lancet 2, 1027-29.

Fontenot, D. S., and Benton, A. L. 1972. "Perception of direction in the right and left visual fields." Neuropsychologia 10, 447-52.

Frank, J., and Levinson, F. 1976. "C-V dysfunction in dysmetric dyslexia." Academic Therapy 12, 251-83.

Galaburda, A. M., LeMay, M., Kemper, T. L., and Geschwind, N. 1978. "Right-left asymmetries in the brain." Science 199, 852-56.

Gardner, H. 1975. The Shattered Mind. New York: Random House.

Geschwind, N. 1965. "Disconnexion syndromes in animals and man." Brain 88, 237-94, 585-644.

Geschwind, N., and Levitsky, W. 1968. "Human brain: Left-right asymmetries in temporal speech region." Science 161, 186-88.

Goldstein, K. 1948. Language and Language Disturbances. New York: Grune and Stratton.

Goodglass, H., and Kaplan, E. 1972. The Assessment of Aphasia and Related Disorders. Philadelphia: Lea and Febiger.

Graham, F. K., and Kendall, B. S. 1960. "Memory-for-Designs Test. Revised general manual." Perceptual and Motor Skills, Monograph Supplement, No. 2-VII, 11, 147-68.

Gray, W. 1963. Gray Oral Reading Test. Indianapolis: Bobbs Merrill.

Gruber, E. 1962. "Reading ability, binocular coordination and the ophthalmograph." Archives of Ophthalmology 67, 183-90.

Hallgren, B. 1950. "Specific dyslexia (congenital word blindness), a clinical and genetic study." Acta Psychiatrica et Neurologica 65, Supplementum.

Halstead, W. C., and Wepman, J. M. 1959. "The Halstead-Wepman Aphasia Screening Test." Journal of Speech and Hearing Disorders 14, 9-15.

Hardyck, C., and Petrinovich, L. 1977. "Left-handedness." Psychological Bulletin 84, 385-99.

Harley, J. P., and Matthews, C. G. 1976. Food Additives and Hyperactivity: A Test of Feingold's Hypothesis. Paper presented to the International Neuropsychological Society Fourth Annual Convention, Toronto.

Harnad, S., Doty, R. W., Goldstein, L., Jaynes, J., and Krauthamer, G. (Eds.). 1977. Lateralization in the Nervous System. New York: Academic Press.

Hartje, W. 1972. "Reading disturbances in the presence of oculomotor disorders." European Neurology 7, 249-64.

Heffner, H. E. 1977. "Effect of auditory cortex ablation on the perception of meaningful sounds." Neuroscience Abstracts 3, 6.

Hermann, K., and Norrie, E. 1958. "Is congenital word blindness a hereditary type of Gerstmann's syndrome?" Monatschrift fur Psychiatrie und Neurologie 136, 59-73.

Hier, D. B., LeMay, M., Rosenburger, P., and Perlo, V. P. 1978. "Developmental dyslexia." Archives of Neurology 35, 90-92.

Hinshelwood, J. 1895. "Wordblindness and visual memory." Lancet 2, 1564-70.

Hinshelwood, J. 1917. Congenital Word Blindness. London: Lewis.

Hochberg, J. 1970. "Components of literacy: Speculations and exploratory research." In Basic Studies in Reading, edited by H. Levin and J. P. Williams. New York: Basic Books.

Hotz, F. C. 1900. "Two cases of a peculiar visual perversion." Ophthalmological Record 9, 12-13.

Huey, H. 1908. The Psychology and Pedagogy of Reading. New York: Macmillan.

Ingvar, D. H., and Risberg, J. 1967. "Increase of regional cerebral blood flow during mental effort in normals and in patients with focal brain disorders." Experimental Brain Research 3, 195-211.

Jackson, E. 1906. "Developmental alexia (congenital word blindness)." American Journal of Medical Science 131, 843-49.

Jackson, R. T., and Pelton, E. W. 1978. "L-dopa treatment of children with hyperactive behavior." Neurology 28, 331.

Jastak, J. F., and Jastak, S. R. 1965. The Wide Range Achievement Test Manual. Wilmington, Del.: Guidance Associates.

Kahn, P. 1963. "Time orientation and reading achievement." Perceptual and Motor Skills 21, 157-58.

Kalverboer, A. F., Coultre, R., and Casaer, P. 1970. "Implications of congenital ophthalmoplegia for the development of visuo-motor functions (illustrated by a case with Moebius syndrome)." Developmental Medicine and Child Neurology 12, 642-45.

Kerschner, J. R. 1977. "Cerebral dominance in disabled readers, good readers, and gifted children: Search for a valid model." Child Development, 48.

Kimura, D. 1961. "Cerebral dominance and the perception of verbal stimuli." Canadian Journal of Psychology 15, 166-71.

Kimura, D. 1966. "Dual functional asymmetry of the brain in visual perception." Neuropsychologia 4, 275-85.

Kinsbourne, M. 1972. "Behavioral analysis of the repetition deficit in conduction aphasia." Neurology 22, 1126-32.

Kinsbourne, M., and MacMurray, J. 1975. "The effect of cerebral dominance on time sharing between speaking and tapping by preschool children." Child Development 46, 240-42.

Kinsbourne, M., and Warrington, E. K. 1962. "A study of finger agnosia." Brain 85, 47-66.

Kinsbourne, M., and Warrington, E. K. 1963. "Developmental factors in reading and writing backwardness." British Journal of Psychology 54, 145-56.

Kinsbourne, M., and Warrington, E. K. 1965. "The developmental Gerstmann syndrome." Archives of Neurology 8, 490-501.

Kirk, S. A., and Bateman, B. 1962. "Diagnosis and remediation of learning disabilities." Exceptional Children 29, 73-78.

Kirk, S. A., McCarthy, J. J., and Kirk, W. D. 1968. Examiner's Manual: Illinois Test of Psycholinguistic Abilities. Urbana, Ill.: University of Illinois Press.

Krippner, S. 1973. "An evaluation of NO procedures on children with brain dysfunction." Academic Therapy 9, 221-29.

Kussmaul, A. 1884. Les Troubles de la parole. Paris: Bailliere.

Launay, C. 1952. "Etude d'ensemble des inaptitudes a la lecture." Seminale Hopitale Paris 35, 1463-74.

Lecours, A. R. 1975. "Myelogenetic correlates of the development of speech and language." In Foundations of Language Development, edited by E. Lenneberg and E. Lenneberg. Vol. 1. New York: Academic Press.

Lee, L. L. 1969. Northwestern Syntax Screening Test. Evanston: Northwestern University Press.

Lesevre, N. 1964. "Les Mouvements oculaires d'exploration: Etude electro-oculographique comparee d'enfants normaux et d'enfants dyslexiques." Unpublished doctoral dissertation, University of Paris.

Lesevre, N. 1966. "Les Mouvements oculaires d'exploration." ICAA Word Blind Bulletin 4, 15-24.

Lesevre, N. 1968. "L'Organisation du regard chez infants d'age scolaire, lecteurs, normaux et dyslexiques." Revue de neuropsychiatrie infantile 16, 323-49.

Levy, J., and Reid, M. 1976. "Variations in writing posture and cerebral organization." Science 194, 337-39.

Luria, A. R. 1966. Higher Cortical Functions in Man. New York: Basic Books.

Mackworth, N., and Morandi, A. 1967. "The gaze selects information details within pictures." Perception and Psychophysics 2, 547-52.

Marcel, T., Katz, L., and Smith, M. 1974. "Laterality and reading proficiency." Neuropsychologia 12, 131-39.

Marcel, T., and Rajan, P. 1975. "Lateral specialization of words and faces in good and poor readers." Neuropsychologia 13, 489-97.

Marie, P. 1906. "Revision de la question de l'aphasie: Le 3e circonvolution frontale gauche ne jove aucun role speciale dans la fonction du langage." Semaine Medicale, May 23, 241-47.

Marie, P. 1971. Pierre Marie's Papers on Speech Disorders. New York: Hafner.

Matin, E. 1974. "Saccadic suppression: A review and an analysis." Psychological Bulletin 81, 899-917.

Mattis, S., French, J., and Rapin, E. 1975. "Dyslexia in children and young adults: Three independent neuropsychological syndromes." Developmental Medicine and Child Neurology 17, 150-63.

McCarthy, J. J., and McCarthy, J. F. 1969. Learning Disabilities. Boston: Allyn and Bacon.

McCready, E. B. 1909-10. "Congenital word blindness as a cause of backwardness in school-children: Report of a case associated with stuttering." American Journal of Psychology 6, 267-77.

Menckes, J. H. 1977. "Early feeding history of children with learning disorders." Developmental Medicine and Child Neurology 19, 169-71.

Milner, E. 1976. "CNS maturation and language acquisition." In Studies in Neurolinguistics, Vol. 1, edited by H. A. Whitaker and H. A. Whitaker. New York: Academic Press.

Mishkin, M., and Forgays, D. G. 1952. "Word recognition as a function of retinal locus." Journal of Experimental Psychology 43, 43-48.

Mohr, J. P. 1976. "Broca's area and Broca's aphasia." In Studies in Neurolinguistics, Vol. 1, edited by H. A. Whitaker and H. A. Whitaker. New York: Academic Press.

Molfese, D., Freeman, R. B., and Palermo, D. S. 1975. "The ontogeny of brain lateralization for speech and nonspeech stimuli." Brain and Language 2, 356-68.

Morgan, W. P. 1896. "A case of congenital word blindness." British Medical Journal 2, 1378.

Mosse, H. L., and Daniels, C. R. 1959. "Linear dyslexia." American Journal of Psychotherapy 13, 826-41.

Murray, H. A. 1938. Explorations in Personality. New York: Oxford University Press.

Myklebust, H. 1965. Disorders of Written Language. New York: Grune and Stratton.

Myklebust, H., and Johnson, D. 1962. "Dyslexia in children." Exceptional Children 29, 14-25.

Nebes, R. D. 1974. "Hemispheric specialization in commissurotomized man." Psychological Bulletin 81, 1-14.

Newcombe, F. 1969. Penetrating Missile Wounds of the Brain. Oxford: Oxford University Press.

Ojemann, G., and Whitaker, H. A. 1978. "The bilingual brain." Archives of Neurology 35, 409-12.

Oldfield, R. C. 1971. "The assessment of handedness: The Edinburgh Inventory." Neuropsychologia 9, 97-113.

Orton, S. T. 1925. "Word blindness in school children." Archives of Neurology and Psychiatry 14, 581-615.

Orton, S. T. 1937. Reading, Writing and Speech Problems in Children. New York: Norton.

Parisi, D., and Pizzamiglio, L. 1970. "Syntactic comprehension in aphasia." Cortex 6, 204-15.

Penfield, W., and Roberts, L. 1958. Speech and Brain Mechanisms. Princeton: Princeton University Press.

Penn, J. M. 1966. "Reading disability: A neurological deficit?" Exceptional Children 33, 243-48.

Peters, A. 1908. "Uber kongenitale wortblindheit." Munchen medinishe wochenschrift 55, 1116-1239.

Pirozzolo, F. J. 1973. "The projective measurement of achievement motivation." Unpublished master's thesis, University of Chicago.

Pirozzolo, F. J. 1977a. "Lateral asymmetrics in visual perception: A review of tachistoscopic visual half-field studies." Perceptual and Motor Skills 45, 695-701.

Pirozzolo, F. J. 1977b. "Visual-spatial and oculomotor deficits in developmental dyslexia: Evidence for two neurobehavioral syndromes of reading disability." Unpublished doctoral dissertation, University of Rochester.

Pirozzolo, F. J. 1978a. "Disorders of perceptual processing." In Handbook of Perception, edited by E. G. Carterette and M. P. Friedman, Vol. 9. New York: Academic Press.

Pirozzolo, F. J. 1978b. "Cerebral asymmetries and reading acquisition." Academic Therapy 13, 261-66.

Pirozzolo, F. J. 1978c. "Slow saccades." Archives of Neurology 35, 618.

Pirozzolo, F. J., and Hess, D. W. 1976. "A neuropsychological analysis of the ITPA: Two profiles of reading disability." Paper presented to the New York State Orton Society Annual Convention, Rochester, New York.

Pirozzolo, F. J., Horner, F., and Okiwara, A. 1978. "Acousticomnestic and linguistic deficits in left temporal lobe agenesis." In press.

Pirozzolo, F. J., and Pirozzolo, P. H. 1978. "A psychometric study of two forms of reading disability." Mimeographed.

Pirozzolo, F. J., and Rayner, K. 1977. "Hemispheric specialization in reading and word recognition." Brain and Language 4, 248-61.

Pirozzolo, F. J.,and Rayner, K. 1978a. "The neural control of eye movements in acquired and developmental reading disorders." In Studies in Neurolinguistics 4, edited by H. A. Whitaker and H. A. Whitaker. New York: Academic Press.

Pirozzolo, F. J., and Rayner, K. 1978b. "Disorders of oculomotor scanning and graphic orientation in developmental Gerstmann syndrome." Brain and Language 5, 119-26.

Pirozzolo, F. J., and Rayner, K. 1979. "Cerebral organization and reading disability." Neuropsychologia 17, in press.

Pirozzolo, F. J., Rayner, K., and Whitaker, H. A. 1977a. "Left hemisphere mechanisms in dyslexia: A neuropsychological case study." Paper presented to the International Neuropsychological Society Fifth Annual Convention, Santa Fe, New Mexico.

Pirozzolo, F. J., Selnes, O. A., Whitaker, H. A., and Horner, F. 1977b. "Linguistic specialization of the left hemisphere." Neuroscience Abstracts 3, 748.

Pontius, A. A. 1976. "Dyslexia and specifically distorted drawings of the face: A new subgroup with prosopagnosia-like signs." Experientia 32, 1432-35.

Prechtl, H. F. R., and Stemmer, J. C. 1959. "Ein choreatiformei syndrom bei kindern." Weiner medinische wochenschrift 109, 461-63.

Purdue Research Foundation. 1948. Examiner's Manual for the Purdue Pegboard. Chicago: Science Research Associates.

Quiros, J. de. 1964. "Dysphasia and dyslexia in school children." Folia Phonetrica 16, 201-22.

Rabinovitch, R. D. 1959. "Reading and learning disabilities." In American Handbook of Psychiatry, Vol. 1, edited by S. Arieti. New York: Basic Books.

Rapin, I., Mattis, S., Rowan, A. J., and Golden, G. 1977. "Verbal auditory agnosia in children." Developmental Medicine and Child Neurology 19, 192-207.

Raven, J. C. 1958. Standard Progressive Matrices. New York: Psychological Corporation.

Raven, J. C. 1962. Coloured Progressive Matrices. New York: Psychological Corporation.

Rayner, K. 1975. "The perceptual span and peripheral cues in reading." Cognitive Psychology 7, 65-81.

Rayner, K. 1977. "Visual attention in reading: Eye movements reflect cognitive processes." Memory and Cognition 5, 443-48.

Rayner, K. 1978a. "Saccadic latencies for parafoveally presented words." Bulletin of the Psychonomic Society 11, 13-16.

Rayner, K. 1978b. "Eye movements in reading and information processing." Psychological Bulletin 85, 618-60.

Rayner, K., and McConkie, G. W. 1976. "What guides a reader's eye movements?" Vision Research 16, 829-37.

Rayner, K., and McConkie, G. W. 1977. "Perceptual processes in reading: The perceptual spans." In Toward a Psychology of Reading, edited by A. Reiber and D. Scarborough. Hillsdale, N.J.: Lawrence Erlbaum Associates.

Rayner, K., and Pirozzolo, F. J. 1978. "Handedness and cerebral dominance as factors in saccadic eye movement latencies." Mimeographed.

Reitan, R. M. 1955. "Certain differential effects of left and right cerebral lesions in human adults." Journal of Comparative and Physiological Psychology 48, 474-77.

Rey, A. 1964. L'Examen clinique on psychologie. Paris: Presses Universitaires de France.

Robbins, M. V., and Glass, G. V. 1969. "The Doman-Delacato rationale: A critical analysis." In Educational Therapy, Vol. 2, edited by J. Hellmuth. Seattle: Special Child Publications.

Robinson, G. H., Koth, B. W., and Ringenbach, J. P. 1976. "Dynamics of the eye and head during an element of visual search." Ergonomics 19, 691-709.

Rourke, B. P. 1976. "Reading retardation in children: Developmental lag or deficit." In The Neuropsychology of Learning Disorders, edited by R. M. Knights and D. J. Bakker. Baltimore: University Park Press.

Rourke, B. P., Dietrich, D. M., and Young, G. C. 1973. "Significance of WISC verbal-performance discrepancies for younger children with learning disabilities." Perceptual and Motor Skills 36, 275-82.

Rourke, B. P., and Telegdy, G. 1971. "Lateralizing significance of WISC verbal performance discrepancies for older children with learning disabilities." Perceptual and Motor Skills 33, 875-83.

Rubino, C. A., and Minden, H. A. 1973. "An analysis of eye movements in children with reading disability." Cortex 9, 217-20.

Rudel, R., and Denckla, M. B. 1974. "Relation of forward and backward digit repetition to neurological impairment in children with learning disabilities." Neuropsychologia 12, 109-18.

Russell, E. W., Neuringer, C., and Goldstein, G. 1970. Assessment of Brain Damage: A Neuropsychological Key Approach. New York: Wiley Interscience.

Rutledge, C. O., Azzaro, A. J., and Ziance, R. J. 1977. "In vitro release of 5-HT with amphetamines." In Advances in Biochemical Psychopharmacology, Vol. 5, edited by E. Costa and M. Sandler. New York: Raven Press.

Rutter, M., Graham, P., and Yule, W. 1970a. "A neuropsychiatric study in childhood." Clinics in Developmental Medicine No. 5, 35/36. London: Heineman.

Rutter, M., Tizard, J., and Whitmore, K., eds. 1970b. Education, Health and Behavior. London: Longmans.

Rutter, M., and Yule, W. 1975. "The concept of specific reading retardation." Journal of Child Psychology and Psychiatry 16, 161-97.

Saffran, E., Schwartz, M., and Marin, O. 1976. "Semantic mechanisms in paralexia." Brain and Language 3, 255-65.

Satz, P. 1976. "Cerebral dominance and reading disability: An old problem revisited." In The Neuropsychology of Learning Disorders, edited by R. M. Knights and D. J. Bakker. Baltimore: University Park Press.

Satz, P., and Friel, J. 1974. "Some predictive antecedents of specific reading disability: A preliminary two-year follow-up." Journal of Learning Disabilities 7, 437-44.

Satz, P., and van Nostrand, G. K. 1973. "Developmental dyslexia: An evaluation of a theory." In The Disabled Learner: Early Detection and Intervention, edited by P. Satz and J. J. Ross. Rotterdam: Rotterdam University Press.

Sechzer, J. A., Folstein, S. E., Geiger, E. H., and Mervis, D. F. 1977. "Effects of neonatal disconnection in kittens." In Lateralization in the Nervous System, edited by S. Harnad, R. W. Doty, L. Goldstein, J. Jaynes, and G. Krauthamer. New York: Academic Press.

Selnes, O. A. 1974. "The corpus callosum: Some anatomical and functional considerations with special reference to language." Brain and Language 1, 111-40.

Selnes, O. A. 1977. "Concurrent cognitive and manual activity as a method for assessing cerebral dominance in normal subjects." Ph.D. dissertation, University of Rochester.

Shetty, T., and Chase, T. N. 1976. "Central monoamines and hyperkinesis of childhood." Neurology 26, 1000-02.

Slosson, R. 1963. Slosson Intelligence Test for Children and Adults. East Aurora, New York: Slosson Educational Publications.

Sobotka, K., and May, J. G. 1977. "Visual evoked potentials and reaction time in normal and dyslexic children." Psychophysiology 14, 18-24.

Spache, G. D. 1963. Diagnostic Reading Scales. Monterey, Cal.: McGraw-Hill.

Spache, G. D. 1976. Investigating the Issues of Reading Disabilities. Boston: Allyn and Bacon.

Sperling, G. 1960. "The information available in brief visual presentations." Psychological Monographs 74, No. 11.

Sperry, R. W., Gazzaniga, M. S., and Bogen, J. E. 1969. "Interhemispheric relationships: The neocortical commissures; syndromes of hemispheric disconnection." In Handbook of Clinical Neurology, edited by P. J. Vinken and G. W. Bruyn. Amsterdam: North Holland.

Spragins, A. B., Lefton, L. A., and Fisher, D. F. 1976. "Eye movements while reading and searching spatially transformed test: A developmental examination." Memory and Cognition 4, 36-42.

Spreen, O., and Benton, A. L. 1969. Neurosensory Center Comprehensive Examination for Aphasia. Victoria, B.C.: Neuropsychology Laboratory, Department of Psychology, University of Victoria.

Stebbins, W., Emmel, A., Heriot, J. T., and Rockowitz, R. J. 1975. "Congenital ophthalmoplegia and school achievement: A case study." Developmental Medicine and Child Neurology 17 237-43.

Stennett, R. G., Smythe, P. C., Pinkney, J., and Fairbairn, A. 1972-73. "The relationship of eye movement measures to psychomotor skills and other elemental skills involved in learning to read." Journal of Reading Behavior 5, 1-13.

Stephenson, S. 1907. "Six cases of congenital word blindness affecting three generations of one family." Ophthalmoscope 5, 482-84.

Swanson, D. E., and Tiffin, J. 1936. "Betts' physiological approach to the analysis of reading disabilities as applied to the college level." Journal of Educational Research 29, 433-48.

Tallal, P. 1978. "An experimental investigation of the role of auditory temporal processing in normal and disordered language development." In Language Acquisition and Language Breakdown: Parallels and Divergencies, edited by A. Caramazza and E. B. Zurif. Baltimore: Johns Hopkins Press.

Taylor, S. E. 1965. "Eye movements in reading: Facts and fallacies." American Educational Research Journal 2, 187-202.

Terman, L. M., and Merrill, M. A. 1960. Stanford-Binet Intelligence Scale. Manual for the third revision-Form L-M. Boston: Houghton-Mifflin.

Thiele, R. 1938. "Zur Kenntnis der knogenitalen Wordblindheit." Monatschrift fur Psychiatrie und Neurologie 99, 371.

Thomas, C. J. 1905. "Congenital word blindness and its treatment." Ophthalmoscope 3, 380-85.

Tinker, M. A. 1958. "Recent studies of eye movements in reading." Psychological Bulletin 55, 215-31.

Trousseau, A. 1877. "De l'Aphasie d'apres les lecons cliniques de Trousseau." In Cliniques Medicales de l'hotel-Dieu de Paris. 5th edition, edited by M. Peters. Paris: Bailliere and Fils.

Van der Abeele, F. 1865. "Observation d'amnesic de lecriture avec conservation de la Parole." Bulletin de l'Academie de Medecine de Belgique 8, 612.

Vernon, M. D. 1957. Backwardness in Reading: A Study of Its Nature and Origin. London: Cambridge University Press.

Wada, J. 1949. "A new method for the determination of the side of cerebral speech dominance: A preliminary report on the intracarotid injection of Sodium Amytal in man." Medical Biology 14, 221-50.

Wada, J. A., Clarke, R., and Hamm, A. 1975. "Cerebral hemispheric asymmetry in humans: Cortical speech zones in 100 adult and 100 infant brains." Archives of Neurology 32, 239-46.

Wender, P. H. 1971. Minimal Brain Dysfunction in Children. New York: Wiley.

Wepman, J. M. 1951. Recovery from Aphasia. New York: Ronald Press.

Wepman, J. M. 1958. Auditory Discrimination Test. Los Angeles: Western Psychological Services.

Wepman, J. M. 1960. "Auditory discrimination, speech and reading." Elementary School Journal 61, 325-33.

Wepman, J. M. 1962. "Dyslexia: Its relationship to language acquisition and concept formation." In Reading Disability: Progress and Research Needs in Dyslexia, edited by J. Money. Baltimore: Johns Hopkins Press.

Wepman, J. M. 1964. "The perceptual basis for learning." In Meeting Individual Differences in Reading, edited by H. A. Robinson. Chicago: University of Chicago Press.

Wepman, J. M. 1965. "The modality concept." Journal of Speech and Hearing Disorders 30, 313-23.

Wepman, J. M., and Morency, A. 1973. Auditory Memory Span Test. Chicago: Language Research Associates.

Wepman, J. M., and Morency, A. 1975. The Auditory Sequential Memory Test. Palm Springs: Language Research Associates.

Wepman, J. M., Morency, A., and Seidl, M. 1975a. The Visual Memory Test. Chicago: Language Research Associates.

Wepman, J. M., Morency, A., and Seidl, M. 1975b. Visual Discrimination Test. Chicago: Language Research Associates.

Wepman, J. M., and Turaids, D. 1975. Spatial Orientation Memory Test. Palm Springs: Language Research Associates.

Wernicke, C. 1874. Der Aphasische symptomenkomplex. Breslau: Cohn and Weigert.

Wernicke, O. 1903. "Cegeura verbal congenita." Revista de la Sociedad Medica Argentina 11, 477-503.

Westheimer, G. H. 1954. "Eye movement responses to a horizontally moving visual stimulus." Archives of Ophthalmology 52, 932-43.

Whitaker, H. A. 1971. On the Representation of Language in the Human Brain. Edmonton: Linguistic Research.

White, C. T., Eason, R. G., and Bartlett, N. R. 1962. "Latency and duration of eye movements in the horizontal plane." Journal of the Optical Society of America 52, 210-13.

White, M. J. 1969. "Laterality differences in perception: A review." Psychological Bulletin 72, 386-405.

Witelson, S. F. 1977. "Neural and cognitive correlates of developmental dyslexia: Age and sex differences." In Psychopathology and Brain Dysfunction, edited by C. Shagass, S. Gershon, and W. Friedhoff. New York: Raven Press.

Witelson, S., and Pallie, W. 1973. "Left hemisphere specialization for language in the newborn: Neuroanatomical evidence of asymmetry." Brain 96, 641-46.

Witty, P. A., and Kopel, D. 1936. "Studies of eye-muscle imbalance and poor fusion in reading disability: An evaluation." Journal of Educational Psychology 27, 663-71.

Woodworth, R. S. 1938. Experimental Psychology. New York: Henry Holt.

Wurtz, R. H., and Mohler, C. W. 1974. "Selection of visual targets for the initiation of saccadic eye movements." Brain Research 71, 209-14.

Yakovlev, P. I., and Lecours, A. R. 1967. "The myelogenetic cycles of regional maturation of the brain." In Regional Development of the Brain in Early Life, edited by A. Minkowski. Oxford: Blackwell.

Yeni-Komshian, G., Isenberg, D., and Goldberg, H. 1975. "Cerebral dominance and reading disability: Left visual field deficit in poor readers." Neuropsychologia 13, 83-94.

Zaidel, D., and Sperry, R. W. 1973. "Performance on Raven's Coloured Progressive Matrices by subjects with cerebral commissurotomy." Cortex 9, 34-39.

Zaidel, E. 1976. "Auditory vocabulary of the right hemisphere following brain bisection or hemidecortication." Cortex 12, 191-211.

Zangwill, O., and Blakemore, C. 1972. "Dyslexia: Reversal of eye movements during reading." Neuropsychologia 10, 371-73.

INDEX

ABOUT THE AUTHOR

FRANCIS J. PIROZZOLO is a Neuropsychologist in the Department of Neurology at the Minneapolis Veterans Administration Hospital. Previously, he was associated with the Department of Psychology, University of California, Los Angeles (UCLA) and the Neurology Service of the Wadsworth Veterans Administration Hospital. Dr. Pirozzolo has published widely in the area of neuropsychology, and his articles have appeared in _Brain and Language_, _Archives of Neurology_, _Neuropsychologia_, _Neuroscience Abstracts_, _Academic Therapy_, and _Perceptual and Motor Skills_. He has edited a book entitled _Neuropsychological and Cognitive Processes in Reading_, which is being published by Academic Press. His book _The Neurological Basis of Behavior_ (Holt, Rinehart and Winston) is scheduled to appear in the near future.

Dr. Pirozzolo holds a B.A. from Wilmington College (Ohio), an M.A. from the University of Chicago, and a Ph.D. from the University of Rochester.

RELATED TITLES
Published by
Praeger Special Studies